SEW MANY GIFTS

19 Handmade Delights to Give or Keep

compiled by KAREN M. BURNS

Create with Confidence

Sew Many Gifts: 19 Handmade Delights to Give or Keep
© 2016 by Martingale & Company®

Martingale®
19021 120th Ave. NE, Ste. 102
Bothell, WA 98011-9511 USA
ShopMartingale.com

Printed in China
21 20 19 18 17 16   8 7 6 5 4 3 2 1

Library of Congress Cataloging-in-Publication Data
is available upon request.

ISBN: 978-1-60468-744-6

MISSION STATEMENT

We empower makers who use fabric and yarn
to make life more enjoyable.

CREDITS

PUBLISHER AND
CHIEF VISIONARY OFFICER
Jennifer Erbe Keltner

CONTENT DIRECTOR
Karen Costello Soltys

MANAGING EDITOR
Tina Cook

ACQUISITIONS EDITOR
Karen M. Burns

TECHNICAL EDITOR
Rebecca Kemp Brent

COPY EDITOR
Sheila Chapman Ryan

PRODUCTION MANAGER
Regina Girard

COVER AND
INTERIOR DESIGNER
Adrienne Smitke

PHOTOGRAPHER
Brent Kane

ILLUSTRATOR
Christine Erikson

Contents

to
WEAR

for the
HOME

for
SEWING
pals

those
on the
GO

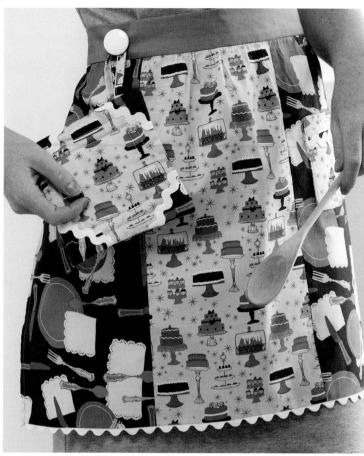

Introduction

• • •

The joy of being a maker is that you don't have to rely on finding the perfect gift at the shopping mall. You can make the perfect gift yourself! But inspiration and occasion aren't always in sync. That's where *Sew Many Gifts* comes in—ready to assist you in your time of inspiration need.

Whether you're on the hunt for just the right birthday present, shower gift, or housewarming gift, or looking to celebrate Mother's Day, a bon voyage party, or simply say thank you to a friend, you'll find just what you're looking for within these pages. And while you'll be able to visualize the many one-of-a-kind treasures you can make, you'll also see several ideas you can imagine whipping up in multiples for group gifts (we even singled out your sewing buddies with their own special section of gifts!). You could even make several gifts ahead to have on hand, ready to wrap and go at a moment's notice.

Best of all, if you're a fabric lover (as most makers are), you'll love the potential each of these gifts holds for personalizing it to match your recipient's personality. The possibilities are endless, and pairing fun fabric choices with functional gifts is a great combination.

Finally, know that we realize some of the very best gifts are the ones we give ourselves: To: Me, From: Me, Love: Me. Go ahead and make as many as you wish for yourself, too. Your secret is safe with us!

Tassel Scarf

This boho-inspired tassel scarf makes a lovely wearable gift, plus it doesn't require knowing the recipient's clothing size or measurements. Choose a lightweight fabric in a pretty print or texture and adorn it with coordinating handmade tassels.

Designed by Beth Bradley

● ● ●

FINISHED SCARF:
40" x 40", excluding tassels

MATERIALS

Yardage is based on 42"-wide fabrics.

1¼ yards of lightweight woven fabric, such as voile or gauze

Lightweight cotton yarn or crochet thread, approximately 40 yards

Hand-sewing needle

Scrap of sturdy cardboard

CUTTING

From the lightweight woven fabric, cut:
1 square, 40½" x 40½"

••• Snag-Free Sewing •••

Lightweight fabrics are delicate, so choose sharp serrated shears and fine pins to avoid snags. Use a fresh machine needle in a smaller size, such as 60/8 or 70/10, and smooth polyester or all-purpose sewing thread.

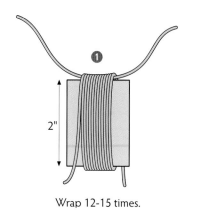

Wrap 12-15 times.

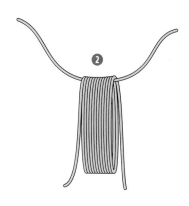

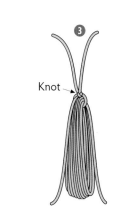

Knot

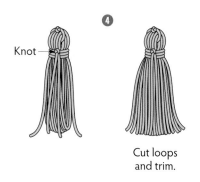

Knot

Cut loops
and trim.

MAKING THE TASSELS

1. Cut a piece of cardboard measuring 1½" x 2" to use as a form. The 2"-long edge runs lengthwise and determines the tassel length. Cut two 8" lengths of yarn to use as ties.

2. Place one tie horizontally on the top edge of the cardboard. Wrap the yarn from the skein around the cardboard lengthwise 12–15 times, beginning and ending at the bottom edge of the cardboard. Cut off the excess yarn. **(1)**

3. Gently slide the loops of yarn and the tie off the cardboard. **(2)**

4. Tie the 8" length of yarn in a secure knot around the bundle of loops, and then fold the ends of the knotted yarn down so that they blend into the tassel. **(3)**

5. Wrap the second tie around the bundle of yarn ⅜" to ½" below the knot to secure the tassel pieces. Tie the ends in a secure knot and let the tails hang down into the tassel. Cut through all of the yarn at the bottom of the loops and trim the ends evenly. Make 18 tassels. **(4)**

••• Nifty Necklace •••

For an easy, speedy accessory, make smaller tassels from embroidery floss and thread them onto a simple chain necklace.

Stitch the tassels along two edges of the scarf by hand.

ASSEMBLING THE SCARF

A narrow or rolled hem is a handy and inconspicuous finish for any lightweight fabric, and also works well for garments, napkins, and tablecloths. If you have a rolled-hem foot for your sewing machine and are comfortable using it, by all means do. If not, follow the steps below to finish the edges of the scarf.

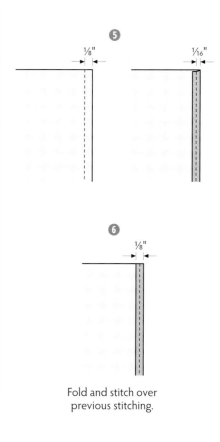

1. Stitch ⅛" from one edge of the fabric square. Fold the edge to the wrong side along the stitches and press. Stitch ⅟₁₆" from the folded edge. (5)

2. Carefully fold ⅛" of the edge to the wrong side again and press. Stitch directly over the previous stitching line from the wrong side of the scarf. The finished hem will be secure and narrow, with only one stitching line visible on the right side of the scarf. Repeat to hem the remaining three edges of the scarf. (6)

3. Measure two opposite edges of the scarf and mark every 5" with a pin. Adjust the spacing of the pins, if necessary, so that they're distributed evenly along the edges. Place a tassel at each pin and corner of the scarf; you'll use nine tassels on each edge. Stitch the top of each tassel securely to the scarf hem with a few hand stitches.

Fold and stitch over previous stitching.

Haute Headbands

Stretchy headbands are so quick to sew that you'll want to make them for all of your granddaughters, girlfriends, sisters, and nieces. Make a trendy turban style or a simpler gathered knot.

Designed by Beth Bradley

• • •

Turban Headband

FINISHED HEADBAND:
22" circumference (stretched) x 5¾" high

MATERIALS

⅓ yard of 58"-wide lightweight knit fabric with at least 50% stretch

Ballpoint or jersey needle

CUTTING

From the knit fabric, cut:
1 rectangle, 12" x 40½" (place the long edges on the crosswise grain)

••• Stretch Test •••

Fifty-percent stretch means that the fabric will stretch crosswise to at least one and a half times its beginning width. To check your fabric's stretch, place two pins in the fabric 4" apart along the crosswise grain. Position the pins away from the cut edges and selvages for the most accurate results. Stretch the fabric; the space between pins must increase to at least 6" for 50% stretch.

You may also want to look for a knit fabric with some spandex content. Spandex improves the recovery, or snapback, of the fabric when it's released after stretching.

Fold.

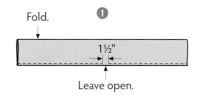

1½"

Leave open.

Align raw edges.

Stitch opening closed.

Twist once.

Twist twice.

Place one loop inside the other.

Stitch center back.

A 40½" length finishes to comfortably fit an average adult head circumference of 22"; adjust as needed for your head size and the stretchiness of your fabric.

ASSEMBLING THE HEADBAND

Stitch with a ¼" seam allowance.

1. Fold the rectangle in half lengthwise with right sides together. Select a stretch stitch or very narrow zigzag stitch on the machine and install a ballpoint or jersey needle. Sew the long edges together, leaving a 1½"-long opening near the center for turning. **(1)**

2. Tuck one end of the tube to the inside as if you are turning the tube right side out. While partially turned, fold it in half crosswise with right sides together, aligning the raw edges at the open ends. Be sure that the tube isn't twisted and that the seam is aligned along its entire length. Sew the ends of the tube together in a circular seam. Find the opening and turn the tube right side out, forming a loop. Turn the seam allowances to the wrong side and slip-stitch the opening closed. Center the lengthwise seam on the inside of the loop, pressing lightly if desired. **(2)**

3. Place the loop horizontally on a flat work surface with the end-joining seam along the fold at one side. Twist all the layers of the headband twice at the center as shown, forming two loops. **(3)**

4. Grasp the twisted center and place one loop inside the other, aligning the edges and forming a turban knot at the top of the headband. **(4)**

5. The end-joining seam should lie at the center back; adjust the fabric tube as necessary if not. Topstitch through all layers at the center back to keep the headband layers aligned when wearing. **(5)**

Knotted Headband

FINISHED HEADBAND: 22" circumference (stretched) x 3¾" high

MATERIALS

¼ yard of 58"-wide lightweight knit fabric with at least
  50% stretch (See "Stretch Test" on page 10.)

Ballpoint or jersey needle

CUTTING

From the knit fabric, cut:
1 rectangle, 8" x 21½"
1 rectangle, 2½" x 3"

ASSEMBLING THE HEADBAND

Stitch with a ¼" seam allowance.

1. Follow steps 1 and 2 for the Turban Headband on page 12 to construct a fabric loop from the large rectangle.

2. Pinch the fabric tube together at the end-joining seam and hand stitch the gathers in place. **(6)**

3. Fold the small rectangle in half lengthwise with right sides together. Stitch the long open edges and turn the little tube right side out. Center the seam on the back of the tube and press lightly. Wrap the small tube around the gathered area of the headband, overlapping the raw ends of the tube on the inside of the headband. Hand stitch the ends of the small tube together, taking a few stitches into the headband to secure the small tube. **(7)**

Left: *Turban headband*

Right: *Knotted headband*

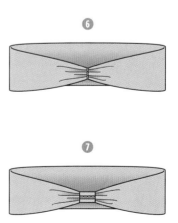

Fat-Quarter Apron & Pot Holder

Make this cute apron for an avid cook or as a wedding-shower or housewarming gift. It requires just three fat quarters, so it's ideal for using stash fabrics. Use scraps from the apron to stitch a matching pot holder that hangs from a handy waistband button.

By Beth Bradley

FINISHED APRON: 18½" x 17½" (at waist, excluding ties)

FINISHED POT HOLDER: 5½" x 5½"

MATERIALS

1 fat quarter *each* of 3 coordinating prints and/or solids (A, B, and C)

1⅛ yards of ⅝"-wide white rickrack

1 button, 1¼" diameter

6" x 6" square of cotton batting

Point turner or chopstick

CUTTING

From fat quarter A, cut:
1 rectangle, 8½" x 17"
2 squares, 6" x 6"
1 rectangle, 5" x 10"
1 rectangle, 1" x 7"

From fat quarter B, cut:
2 rectangles, 7½" x 17"
4 squares, 2" x 2"

From fat quarter C, cut:
4 strips, 4" x 19"

••• Best Batting •••

Always choose 100% cotton batting or batting designed for kitchen use when you're making projects that will be subjected to heat. Synthetic battings may melt.

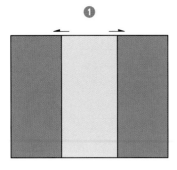

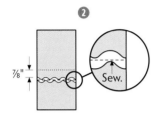

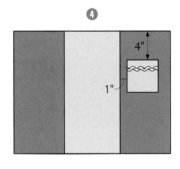

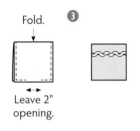

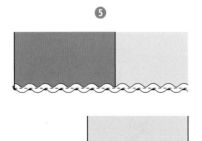

ASSEMBLING THE APRON

Stitch with a ¼" seam allowance unless otherwise noted.

1. Sew a B rectangle to each long edge of the 8½" x 17" A rectangle. Use a serger, zigzag, or overcasting stitch to finish the edges. Press the seam allowances toward the B rectangles. **(1)**

2. Fold the 5" x 10" A rectangle in half widthwise with wrong sides together; press and then unfold. Cut a 5" length of rickrack and place it on the fabric's right side, ⅞" below the crease; pin. Sew the rickrack in place by stitching along the lengthwise center of the rickrack. **(2)**

3. To make the pocket, refold the rectangle along the original fold line with right sides together. Stitch the open edges, leaving a 2" opening along the bottom for turning. Trim the corners diagonally and turn the unit right side out. Use a point turner to work the edges and corners into place. Press the pocket. **(3)**

4. Pin the pocket right side up on the step 1 apron unit, 4" below the top edge and 1" to the right of the right-hand seam. Edgestitch the sides and bottom edge, closing the opening left for turning as you sew. Leave the top of the pocket open. **(4)**

5. Cut a 22½" length of rickrack. Press ¼" to the wrong side on the bottom edge of the apron. Place the rickrack on the apron's right side along the bottom edge, with the center of the rickrack slightly above the folded fabric edge. Sew along the lengthwise centerline of the rickrack. Fold the apron's folded edge to the wrong side, flipping one edge of the rickrack out to extend below the apron, and press thoroughly. Topstitch ¼" from the bottom fold to secure the rickrack and hem. **(5)**

6. Press ¼" to the wrong side twice along each side edge of the apron. Sew close to the first fold to secure the hems.

7. Set your machine for a long stitch (4.0 to 5.0 mm). Sew ⅛" from the apron top edge, leaving long thread tails at each end.

8. Press ¼" to the wrong side on each short end of one 4" x 19" C strip; this is the waistband. Finger-press the apron and waistband to find the centers of the top edges. Place the waistband on the apron with right sides together, matching the

centers and side edges, and pin. Gently pull the bobbin threads to gather the top edge to fit the waistband, distributing the gathers evenly. Sew the top edge. Press the seam allowances toward the waistband. **(6)**

9. Press ¼" to the wrong side on the long raw edge of the waistband. Fold the waistband lengthwise with wrong sides together, aligning the pressed edge ⅛" below the waist seamline on the wrong side, and pin, concealing the seam allowances inside the waistband. From the apron right side, stitch in the ditch of the waist seamline, catching the fold on the wrong side as you sew. **(7)**

10. Cut one of the C strips in half. Stitch a half-strip to one end of each remaining C strip to make the waist ties. Press the seam allowances open. Fold each tie in half lengthwise with right sides together and sew the long open edge and one short edge. Trim the corners diagonally. Turn each tie right side out using a point turner and press.

11. Slip the raw end of one tie into the opening at one side of the waistband, overlapping the ends by ½". Topstitch ¼" from the pressed waistband edge to secure the tie end. Repeat to insert the second tie into the other side of the waistband. **(8)**

ASSEMBLING THE POT HOLDER

1. Place a 2" B square on each corner of one 6" A square, right sides together. Sew across each B square diagonally from corner to corner as shown. Trim the seam allowances to ¼" wide. Press the seam allowances and triangles toward the corners to make a Snowball block. **(9)**

2. Cut four pieces of rickrack, 3" long. Center one piece over each diagonal seam and topstitch along the lengthwise center of the rickrack.

3. Press ¼" to the wrong side on each long edge of the 1" x 7" A rectangle. Fold the rectangle in half lengthwise with wrong sides together, matching the pressed edges, and press again. Stitch ⅛" from the long open edge to make the pot-holder loop. Fold the loop in half widthwise. Place the loop on the top edge of the pot holder, 1½" from the right edge, with the raw edges of

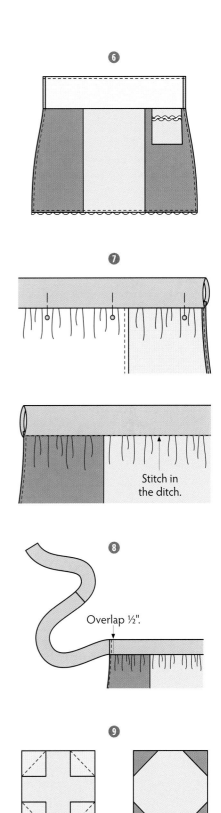

Stitch in
the ditch.

Overlap ½".

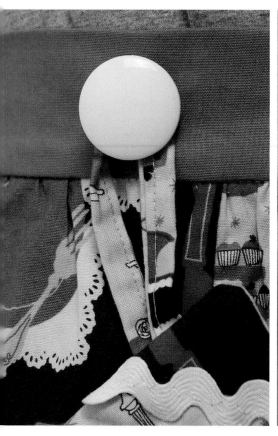

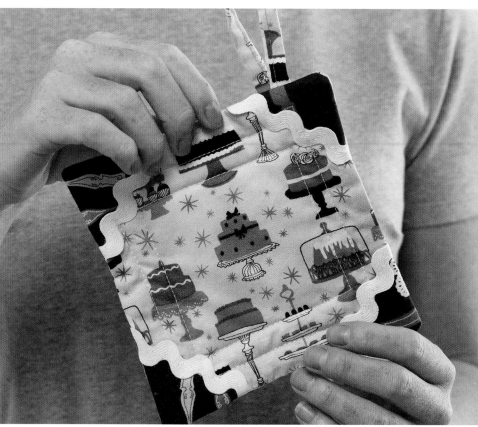

A coordinating pot holder attaches to the apron with a button.

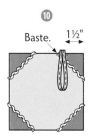

⑩

Baste. 1½"

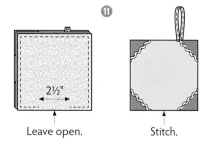

⑪

2½"

Leave open.   Stitch.

the loop extending ¼" beyond the block edge. Stitch ⅛" from the block's raw edge to baste the ends in place. **(10)**

4. Place the remaining A square on the Snowball block with right sides together and top with the batting square. Sew around all four sides, leaving a 2½" opening at the middle of the bottom edge for turning. Trim the corners diagonally and turn the pot holder right side out, smoothing the corners into place with a point-turning tool. Press the pot holder thoroughly, turning the seam allowances to the wrong side along the opening. Press the hanging loop away from the pot holder. Hand stitch the opening closed. **(11)**

5. Quilt the pot holder as desired. The featured pot holder uses straight lines to frame the motif in the center of the fabric.

6. Sew the button to the apron waistband 5" to the left of the center front. Use the button to hang the pot holder by its loop so it's always at hand.

Kitty Pals

The little ones in your life will love these huggable feline friends. Make them from cozy fleece and accessorize your kitty with a necktie or a collar and ruffled dress.

By Beth Bradley

● ● ●

FINISHED KITTY:
approximately 22" x 25", including arms, ears, and legs

MATERIALS

Instructions are for the kitty with ruffled dress and collar, with optional pieces listed. Change the fabrics and colors as desired for variations.

½ yard of 58"-wide light-blue fleece for body

12" x 12" square of white felt for muzzle, stripes, inner ears, and collar (optional)

9" x 12" rectangle of 45"-wide pink print for clothing/body (*or* 11" x 14" with optional ruffle)

1½" x 3" piece of black felt for eyes

1½" x 1½" piece of brown felt for nose

3" x 6" piece of blue felt for necktie (optional)

Polyester fiberfill

6-strand embroidery floss in black

CUTTING

Patterns and embroidery design are on pages 24–25.

From the light-blue fleece, cut:
1 rectangle, 10½" x 16"
1 rectangle, 8½" x 10½"
4 arms
4 legs
4 ears

From the pink print, cut:
1 rectangle, 8" x 10½"
1 rectangle, 2" x 13" (optional; for ruffle)

From the white felt, cut:
1 muzzle, *on fold*
2 inner ears
1 large stripe
2 small stripes
2 collars (optional)

From the black felt, cut:
2 eyes

From the brown felt, cut:
1 nose

From the blue felt (optional, for necktie), cut:
1 knot
1 tie

Customize your kitty with different fabrics and accessories.

PREPARING THE PIECES

Stitch with a ¼" seam allowance unless otherwise noted.

1. Place the muzzle and stripes on the 8½" x 10½" fleece rectangle as shown, allowing ½" between stripes; pin. Edgestitch the long edges of the stripes and the top edge of the muzzle with matching thread. Center the inner ears on two fleece ears; pin. Edgestitch the long sides of the inner ears. (1)

2. Place the nose and eyes on the face, referring to the photo on page 20 for placement, and pin. Edgestitch the nose and eyes with matching threads. Transfer the mouth and whiskers onto the muzzle using tracing paper or your favorite method. Embroider the mouth and whiskers with a backstitch using two strands of black embroidery floss. If desired, backstitch short curved lines on the outer edges of the eyes for eyelashes. (2)

3. Place the collar pieces along the top of the 8" x 10½" print rectangle and pin. Edgestitch the curved edge using a zigzag stitch and contrasting thread. *Optional:* To substitute a necktie, center the felt knot and tie pieces on the 8" x 10½" print rectangle as shown and pin. Edgestitch the perimeter of each piece. Topstitch diagonal stripes on the tie if desired. (3)

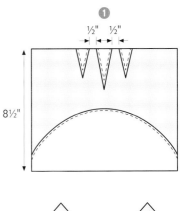

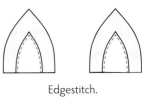

Edgestitch.

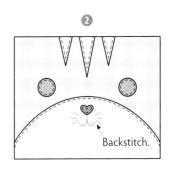

Backstitch.

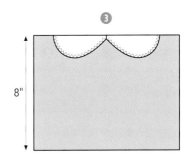

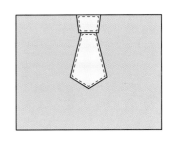

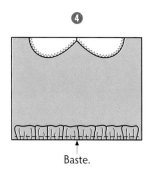

Baste.

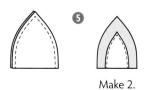

Make 2.

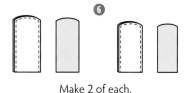

Make 2 of each.

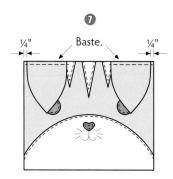

¼"   Baste.   ¼"

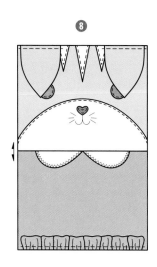

4. To make the optional ruffle, fold the 2" x 13" print rectangle in half lengthwise with right sides together; press. Sew the short edges and turn the strip right side out, matching the raw edges; press. Set the machine for a long stitch (4.0 to 5.0 mm) and sew a scant ¼" from the raw edges, leaving long thread tails on each end. Fold the body and ruffle in half to find and crease the centerlines. Pin the ruffle to the bottom edge of the body, aligning the raw edges and matching the centerlines. Align the short ends of the ruffle ¼" from each side edge of the body rectangle and pin. Gently pull the bobbin threads to gather the ruffle to fit the body rectangle, leaving ¼" of the body free on each end. Baste the ruffle to the body by stitching ¼" from the raw edges. (4)

5. Pin one ear unit from step 1 to one of the plain fleece ears, right sides together. Stitch the curved edges, leaving the short, straight edge open. Clip the seam allowances along the curves and turn the ear right side out; press lightly. Make two ears. (5)

6. Place two legs right sides together. Stitch the long edges and curved edge, leaving the short straight edge open. Clip the seam allowances along the curves and turn the leg right side out. Stuff the leg with fiberfill until plump. Make two legs; repeat the entire step to make two arms. (6)

7. Place the ears ¼" from the top corners of the face with right sides together, aligning the raw edges. Baste the ears in place. (7)

ASSEMBLING THE CAT

1. Sew the top of the body to the bottom edge of the face with right sides together. Press the seam allowances open. (8)

> ### ••• Custom Cat •••
>
> This is an ideal project for using fun scraps from your stash, as well as leftover buttons, trim, and ribbon from past projects. Give your kitty a fancy rickrack-trimmed collar or front pocket, or embroider the recipient's initials on the necktie.

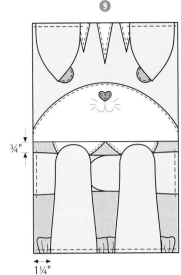

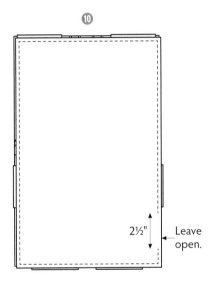

2. Place the arms on the sides of the body ¾" below the seam, aligning the raw edges, and pin. Pin the legs to the bottom edge of the body 1¼" from the corners, aligning the raw edges. Baste the raw edges of the arms and legs to the body. (9)

3. Place the large rectangle on the assembled front, right sides together and tucking the arms and legs between the layers. Pin the perimeter, making sure the arms, legs, ears, and ruffle stay between the layers. The arms and legs are bulky, so match the edges of the front and back carefully and pin generously. Be sure the ears and the finished ends of the ruffle are at least ¼" from the side edges so that they don't get caught in the side seams. Sew around all four sides of the body, leaving a 2½" opening for turning along one side. (10)

4. Trim the seam allowances diagonally at the corners to reduce bulk. Carefully turn the cat right side out through the opening, turning the ears, arms, and legs away from the body. Fill the body with fiberfill until plump. Finger-press the seam allowances to the wrong side along the opening and then slip-stitch the opening closed. (11)

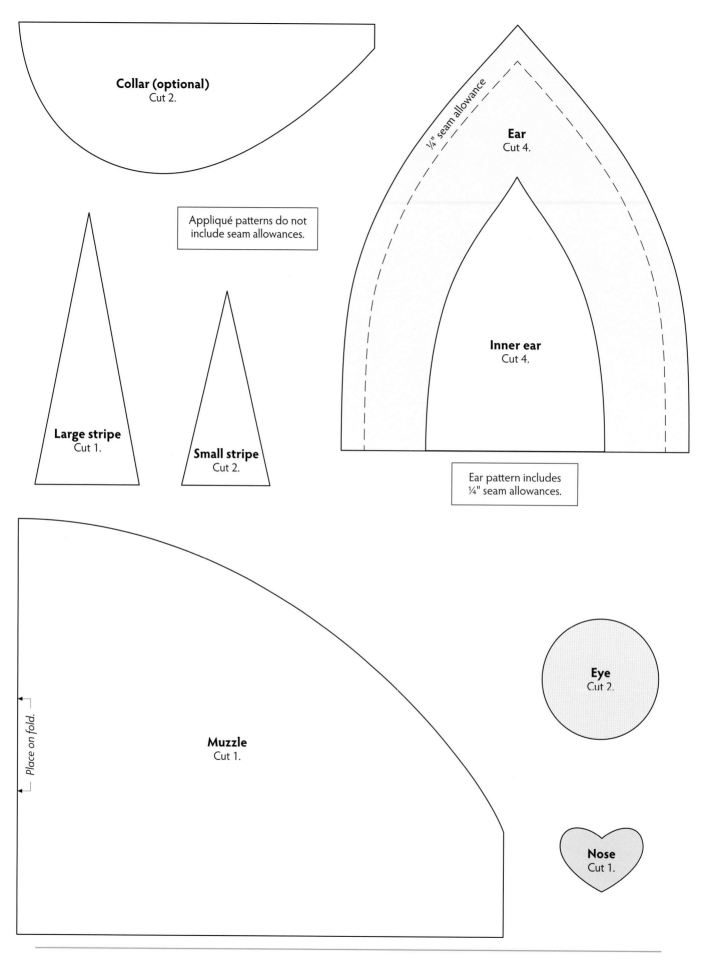

Collar (optional)
Cut 2.

Ear
Cut 4.

¼" seam allowance

Appliqué patterns do not include seam allowances.

Large stripe
Cut 1.

Small stripe
Cut 2.

Inner ear
Cut 4.

Ear pattern includes ¼" seam allowances.

Place on fold.

Muzzle
Cut 1.

Eye
Cut 2.

Nose
Cut 1.

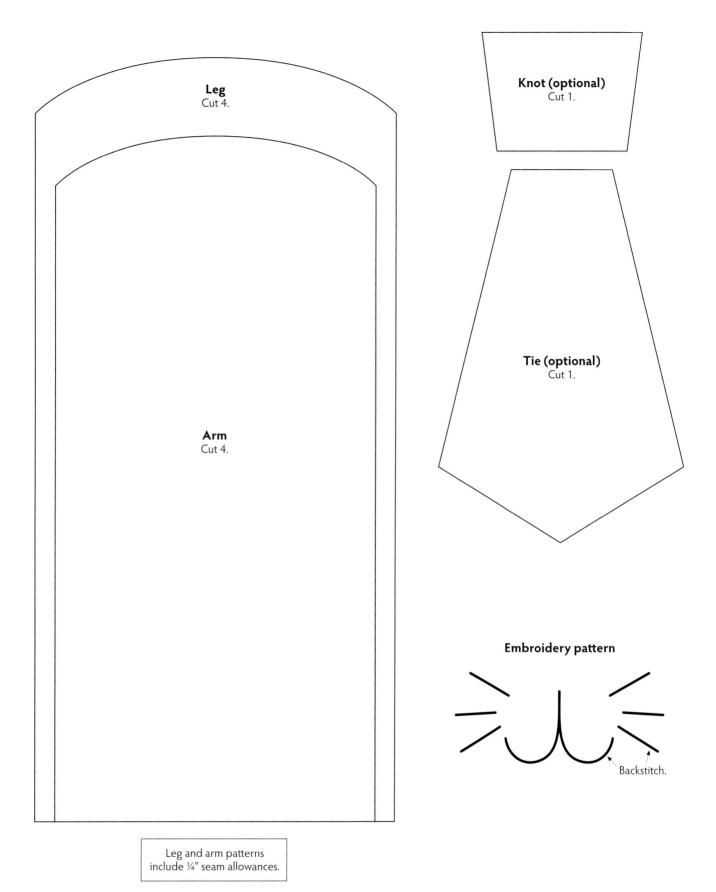

Leg
Cut 4.

Arm
Cut 4.

Knot (optional)
Cut 1.

Tie (optional)
Cut 1.

Embroidery pattern

Backstitch.

Leg and arm patterns
include ¼" seam allowances.

Burlap Chalkboard Banner

Banners announcing a special event are always fun. The best part about this banner is the chalkboard fabric: it's easy to change the celebratory message! Make your banner multipurpose with neutral colors, or make a separate banner with fun, vibrant colors for each occasion.

By Sarah M. Bisel

● ● ●

FINISHED BANNER: 130" x 6½"

FINISHED FLAG: 5" x 6½"

MATERIALS

Instructions are for 1 banner with 10 flags.

½ yard of 42"-wide natural-colored burlap

¼ yard of 48"-wide chalkboard fabric

6 squares, 5" x 5", of assorted prints

¼ yard of red print for binding

CUTTING

Patterns A and B are on page 30.

From the burlap, cut:
2 strips, 6½" x 42"; crosscut into 10 rectangles, 5" x 6½". Use pattern A to mark and trim the lower edge of each rectangle.

From the chalkboard fabric, cut:
1 strip, 5½" x 42"; crosscut into 10 rectangles, 4" x 5½". Use pattern B to mark and trim the lower edge of each rectangle.

From the red print, cut:
4 strips, 2" x 42"

Make reusable banners with write-on, wipe-off chalkboard fabric.

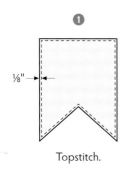

① Topstitch.

⅛"

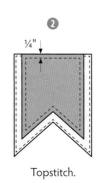

Topstitch.

¼"

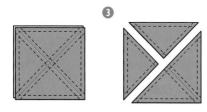

②

Topstitch.

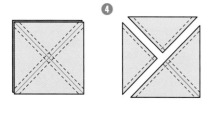

③

④

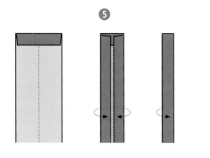

Trim. → Turn and press.

⑤

ASSEMBLING THE FLAGS

1. Topstitch each burlap flag ⅛" from the raw edges to prevent fraying. Burlap frays quickly and easily, so handle the flags as little as possible before stitching to minimize the fraying. **(1)**

2. Center each chalkboard flag on top of a burlap flag, matching the raw edges at the top and aligning the peaks at the bottom. Topstitch ¼" from the edges of each chalkboard flag. **(2)**

3. You can make the smaller triangular flags with either raw or finished edges.

   Raw-edge instructions: Pair the six assorted squares with *wrong* sides together. Draw two diagonal lines from corner to corner on the top square in each pair, making an X. Topstitch ¼" from both sides of each line, and then topstitch around the perimeter of the square, ¼" from the raw edges. Repeat with each pair of 5" squares. Cut on the marked lines to make four triangles from each pair (12 total; 1 will be left over). **(3)**

   Finished-edge instructions: Pair the six assorted squares with *right* sides together. Draw two diagonal lines from corner to corner on the top square in each pair, making an X. Sew ¼" from both sides of each line. Repeat with each pair of 5" squares. Cut on the drawn lines to make four triangles from each pair (12 total; 1 will be left over). Trim the seam allowances at the apex of each triangle to reduce bulk. Turn the triangles right side out and press. **(4)**

ASSEMBLING THE BANNER

1. Sew the 2"-wide red-print strips together end to end to make a continuous strip. Cut a 131" length for the binding. Press ½" to the wrong side on each short end. Fold the strip in half lengthwise, wrong sides together, and press. Open the fold and press both raw edges to the wrong side so that they meet at the center crease. Refold along the center crease and press once more. **(5)**

> **••• Working with Chalkboard Fabric •••**
>
> Read the instructions for your chalkboard fabric. Each fabric is a little different, and some require preparation to ensure erasability before you can write on them.

Make your spacer triangles with raw or finished edges.

2. Find the center of the prepared binding and mark it with a pin. Arrange the flags and triangles along the length of the binding. Position a small triangle at the center and each end, and alternate flags and triangles. Arrange the pieces so that their side edges abut. You'll have extra binding at each end. **(6)**

3. Slip each triangle and flag into the folded binding. Be sure the raw edge at the top of each flag and triangle rests against the center fold line of the binding. Pin or clip each flag and triangle in place. Note that pinholes in the chalkboard fabric are permanent, so pin only the other fabrics or use clips.

4. Starting at one end of the binding, sew a scant ⅛" from the long open edge of the binding through all the layers. Be sure to catch the folded edge on the back of the binding as well as the other layers. Backstitch the seam at each end to secure. **(7)**

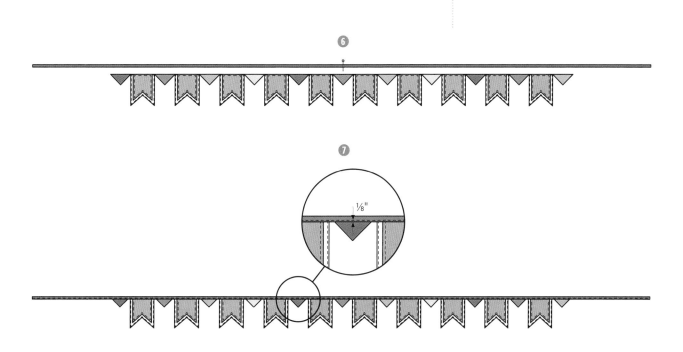

6

7

⅛"

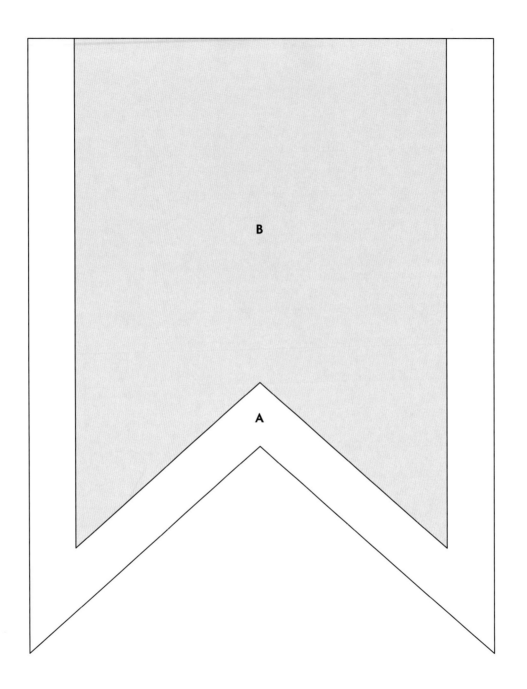

Kitchen Corner

A small project is a fun way to play with color and fabrics while making something new to decorate your space. To give your quilt some depth and make it interesting, choose scrappy fabrics in varying shades and prints within each color family

By Amy Smart

• • •

FINISHED QUILT: 36½" x 36½"

MATERIALS

Yardage is based on 42"-wide fabrics unless otherwise noted.

36 squares, 6¼" x 6¼", of assorted pink, gold, and blue prints for blocks

½ yard of cream print for blocks

⅜ yard of gold stripe for binding

1⅛ yards of fabric for backing

40" x 40" piece of batting

CUTTING

Cut each 6¼" print square in half diagonally to create 72 triangles.

From the cream print, cut:
9 strips, 1½" x 42"; crosscut into 36 rectangles, 1½" x 10"

From the gold stripe, cut:
2½"-wide bias strips totaling at least 154" when joined

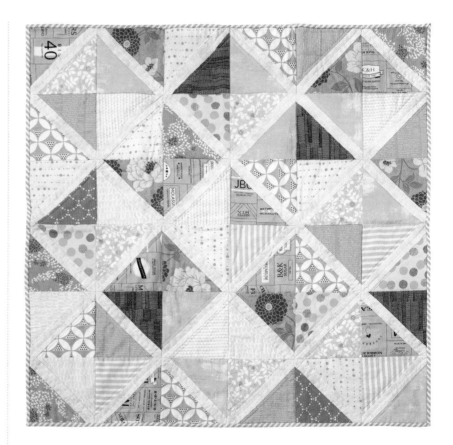

••• Straighten Up •••

If you're using a diagonal stripe or prefer a straight-grain binding, cut four crosswise strips, 2½" x 42", from the gold stripe.

MAKING THE BLOCKS

For each block, choose two contrasting triangles and one 1½" x 10" cream rectangle.

1. Fold the triangles and rectangle in half to find their centerlines and finger-press. Sew the long edge of a triangle to one long edge of the cream rectangle, matching the centers. Press the seam allowances toward the cream strip. Repeat to sew a contrasting triangle to the opposite edge of the same cream rectangle. Make 36 blocks. **(1)**

2. Trim each block to measure 6½" x 6½", keeping the cream rectangles centered. **(2)**

ASSEMBLING THE QUILT

1. Arrange the blocks in six rows of six blocks each, rotating the blocks as shown to create a lattice pattern.

2. Sew the blocks together in rows. Press the seam allowances to the left in odd-numbered rows and to the right in even-numbered rows.

3. Sew the rows together and press the seam allowances in one direction. **(3)**

FINISHING THE QUILT

1. Layer the quilt top, batting, and backing; baste the layers together.

2. Quilt as desired. The sample is stitched in the ditch along the horizontal and vertical block grid, with diagonal lines echoing the cream rectangles.

3. Trim the backing and batting to match the quilt top.

4. Join the striped strips into a continuous length and use it to bind the quilt.

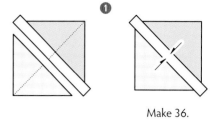

Make 36.

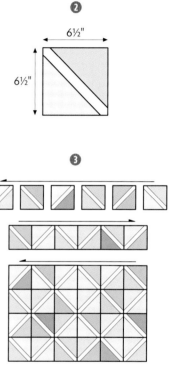

Quilt assembly

Taggie Blanket for Baby

Babies like to touch everything, and in their little worlds, almost everything is a textural sensation. Why not play to that strength with a little play mat or lap blanket for baby to explore and touch?

By Jennifer Keltner

● ● ●

FINISHED BLANKET: 15½" x 23"

MATERIALS

3 squares, 8" x 8", of cotton jersey knit in pink, black, and green polka dots

12 squares, 4¼" x 4¼", of assorted gray cotton polka dots, stripes, and checks

¾ yard of pink dotted plush fabric (such as Shannon Cuddle)

1 square, 3" x 3", of animal-theme print, fussy cut to feature an animal

1 square, 3" x 3", of lightweight fusible web

¼ yard *each* of 1½"-wide rickrack in pink and orange

Scraps of assorted ribbons and trims, at least 4½" long*

2 squares, 4" x 4", of crinkle material (optional; made specifically for baby toys)

The sample uses twill tape, satin ribbon, grosgrain ribbon, decorative-edge binding, and ruffled elastic.

CUTTING

From the plush fabric, cut:
1 rectangle, 18" x 26"
1 rectangle, 4½" x 9"

ASSEMBLING THE QUILT

1. On a flat work surface, lay out the assorted gray cotton 4¼" squares in three Four Patch block

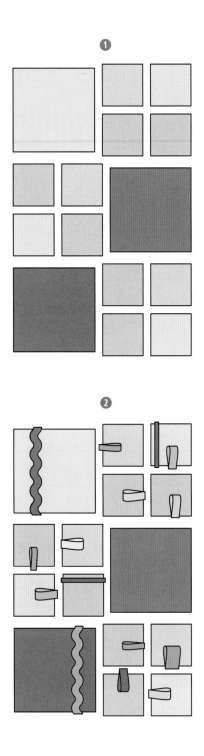

arrangements. Add the three knit polka-dot squares to the layout, alternating them with the Four Patch blocks as shown. **(1)**

2. Cut the assorted trims into 3½" to 4¼" lengths. Fold each in half and arrange as desired on the fabric squares, creating "taggies" that will emerge from various seams on the quilt top. Align the raw edges of the folded trims with the edges of the squares and then vary the lengths by sliding the raw ends of some loops deeper into the seam allowances to shorten the length of the loop visible in the finished blanket. Pin the loops in place.

3. Place pieces of rickrack on the green and pink knit squares as shown. Position the rickrack off-center to avoid bulky seam intersections with the Four Patch blocks. Add strips of trim along the seamlines of some blocks if desired, placing them so that one long edge of the trim will be captured in the seam. **(2)**

4. When you're pleased with the arrangement, sew together each Four Patch block in the order that best allows you to stitch the taggies in place. When pairs of 4¼" squares are sewn together, press the seam allowances away from the desired direction of the included taggies so the loops will lie flat against the blanket. When joining block pairs to complete the Four Patch blocks, it may be necessary to clip the central seam intersection so that all of the taggies lie in the desired directions.

5. Using matching thread, secure the rickrack pieces by sewing two or three rows of straight stitch along the center of each rickrack strip. Trim the ends of the rickrack pieces to match the fabric edges.

6. Join each Four Patch block to the adjacent knit square, keeping in mind that you may have taggies sewn into these seams as well. To prevent stretching, use a walking foot and sew with the knit fabrics against the throat plate of the machine.

7. Join the three pairs of blocks, inserting taggies as planned. Press the seam allowances to position the taggies correctly, clipping the seam allowances as necessary.

8. To make the plush flap, fold the 4½" x 9" rectangle in half with right sides together to make a 4½" square. Sew along two opposite sides using a ¼" seam allowance. Trim the corners diagonally to reduce bulk and turn the flap right side out through the open edge; finger-press. *Optional:* slip two 4" squares of crinkle paper inside the pocket so that the flap will have a crinkly sound when baby touches it.

9. Center the pocket flap on the black polka-dot square with the raw edges of the pocket toward the top of the blanket. Cover the raw edges of the flap with a 4½"-long piece of trim, wrapping the trim ends around the side edges of the flap to hide the ends of the trim beneath the flap. Pin in place. With matching thread, sew two or three rows of zigzag stitches through all the layers to secure the trim and flap to the quilt top.

10. Following the manufacturer's instructions, apply fusible web to the wrong side of the fussy-cut animal motif. Remove the paper backing. Lift the flap and center the motif beneath the flap. Fuse the motif to the blanket and edgestitch in place.

FINISHING THE BLANKET

1. Center the assembled blanket on the large plush rectangle, wrong sides together. Using a walking foot and matching threads, stitch in the ditch along all of the seamlines in the quilt top. Stitch two rows of straight stitches along the center of each rickrack piece. Straight stitch around the fused animal motif beneath the flap.

2. Trim the plush fabric only, leaving 1" extending beyond all four edges of the quilt top. Measure, mark, and cut away a ¾" square of plush fabric at each corner. **(3)**

3. Finger-press ½" to the wrong side twice on one long edge of the plush fabric to cover the raw edges of the quilt top and create a self binding. Pin or clip the binding in place. Straight stitch the binding in place near the interior fold through all layers. Repeat with the opposite long edge, then the top and bottom edges. Fold the raw edges to the wrong side as necessary at the corners, where the squares removed in the previous step will reduce the bulk.

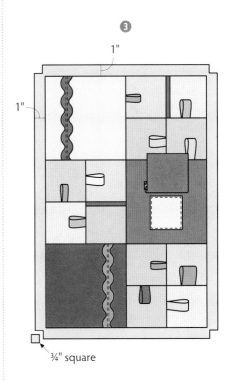

Lift the flap for a game of peekaboo.

¾" square

Bloom Pillow

Choose two values of your favorite color plus a contrasting shade to create this happy pillow. Fusible appliqué makes it a quick and easy project.

By Andy Knowlton

●●●

FINISHED PILLOW: 16" x 16"

MATERIALS

Yardage is based on 42"-wide fabrics unless otherwise noted.

½ yard of white solid for pillow front and back

½ yard of muslin for pillow-top lining

⅛ yard of bright-pink print for outer petals

⅛ yard of dark-pink print for inner petals

4" x 4" scrap of green print for flower center

17" x 17" piece of low-loft batting

⅜ yard of 20"-wide paper-backed fusible web

16" x 16" pillow form

CUTTING

From the white solid, cut:
1 square, 16½" x 16½"
2 rectangles, 11½" x 16½"

From the muslin, cut:
1 square, 17" x 17"

●●● **Spice It Up** ●●●

If you prefer, use scraps rather than purchasing yardage for the flower petals. Choose prints and solids from the same color family, using the darker fabrics for the inner petals and lighter values for the outer petals.

PREPARING THE PILLOW FRONT

1. Trace eight *each* of the inner and outer petals and one flower center (on page 40) onto the paper side of the fusible web, allowing ½" between shapes. Roughly cut out each shape, leaving about ¼" around each piece. Follow the manufacturer's instructions to iron the fusible web onto the wrong side of the corresponding flower fabric. Using sharp scissors, cut out each shape directly on the line. Remove the paper backing.

2. Fold the white 16½" square in half lengthwise and crosswise and finger-press to mark the centerlines. Unfold the square and position the flower pieces on the right side of the pillow front using the fold lines as a guide. Begin by centering the flower center at the folds' intersection and work outward, leaving small, consistent gaps between petals. When you're satisfied with the appliqué placement, fuse the pieces to the pillow front. **(1)**

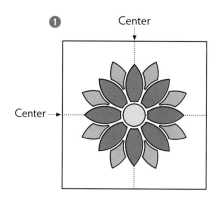

3. Make a quilt sandwich from the squares of muslin and batting and the pillow front; pin or spray baste to hold the layers together. Stitch around the appliqués with coordinating thread and a straight stitch placed about ⅛" from the raw edges, beginning with the center circle and working outward. Continue quilting the pillow top by stitching in the negative space around the flower as desired; the sample uses free-form stippling.

4. Trim the muslin and batting even with the pillow top.

ASSEMBLING THE PILLOW

1. Press ½" to the wrong side *twice* on one long edge of each 11½" x 16½" rectangle. Stitch ⅛" from the first fold to hem the backing rectangles.

2. Place one backing rectangle on the pillow front, right sides together and matching the raw edges at one side. Add the second pillow backing, matching it to the raw edges at the opposite side of the pillow front. The hemmed edges will overlap near the center of the pillow. Pin the pieces together all the way around the outside edge. Stitch using a ¼" seam. Trim the seam allowances diagonally at each corner to reduce bulk. (2)

3. Turn the pillow right side out through the opening in the backing and insert the pillow form.

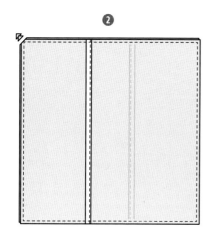

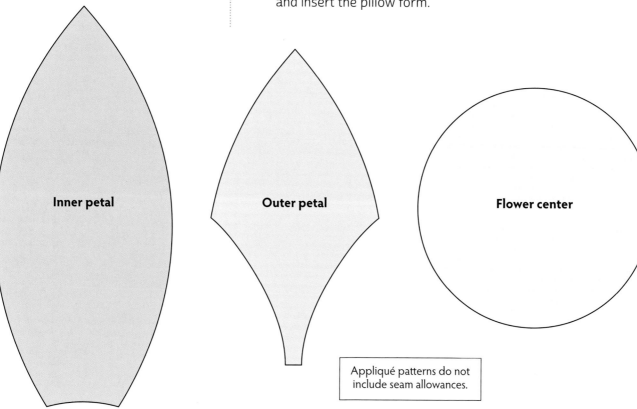

Inner petal

Outer petal

Flower center

Appliqué patterns do not include seam allowances.

Hexie Set

These generously sized mug rugs are perfect for oversized latte cups, or can accommodate regular mugs with room left for a biscuit. Pair them with an embellished kitchen towel and you've got the perfect gift for any coffee or tea lover.

By Adrienne Smitke

• • •

FINISHED MUG RUGS: 6½" x 6½"

FINISHED TEA TOWEL: 19" x 29"

MATERIALS

Yardage is based on 42"-wide fabrics. Materials are for 2 mug rugs and 1 towel.

Assorted scraps, at least 2½" x 2½" each, of purple, gray, and aqua solids and prints for hexagons

⅝ yard of gray linen for mug-rug backing and towel

¼ yard of black-and-white stripe for mug-rug background and towel cuff

¼ yard of magenta solid for binding

2 pieces, 7" x 7", of batting

46 paper hexagon templates, 1"

CUTTING

From the gray linen, cut:
1 rectangle, 20½" x 30½"
2 squares, 7" x 7"

From the black-and-white stripe, cut:
1 rectangle, 6" x 20½"
2 squares, 7" x 7"

From the magenta solid, cut:
2 strips, 2¼" x 42"

••• Fast Forms •••

You can use the pattern on page 45 to prepare your own hexagon templates, or speed the process by purchasing ready-to-use 1" templates from www.paperpieces.com.

PREPARING THE HEXAGONS

1. Using the purple, gray, and aqua scraps, prepare 46 hexagons. Refer to "English Paper Piecing Hexagons" on page 44.

2. Arrange seven assorted hexagons as shown to form a flower and stitch together. Make two. **(1)**

3. Referring to the diagram, arrange the remaining 32 assorted hexagons in five long, interlocking rows. Hand sew the hexagons together. **(2)**

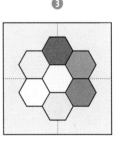

Make 2.

> ### ••• Make Contact •••
>
> Once you've arranged your hexagons, carefully transfer them to a cookie sheet or large tray covered in contact paper, sticky side up, with the paper backing removed. This will keep the pieces in place, making it easy to store them while you work.

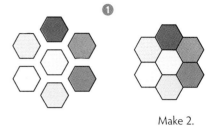

ASSEMBLING THE MUG RUGS

1. Fold a black-and-white 7" square in half vertically and horizontally, finger-pressing each fold to mark the center. Use these creases to center a hexie flower on the block. Pin to secure, and then hand stitch or machine appliqué the flower to the block. Make two. **(3)**

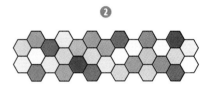

Make 2.

2. Layer an appliquéd block, a batting square, and a linen square. Baste or pin the layers together; machine quilt as desired. Adrienne quilted in the ditch around the outside of the hexagons, and then quilted straight lines across the background. Trim the quilted mat to 6½" x 6½", keeping the flower centered. Make two.

3. Use one magenta strip to bind the outer edges of each mug rug.

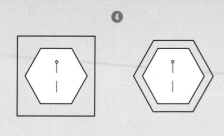

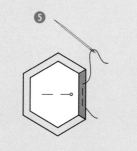

1. Make sure your fabric scraps are *at least* ¼" larger on all sides than the paper template. To save time, you can precut scraps into 2½" squares that will fit the 1" hexagons in this project. The seam allowance need not be even all the way around.

2. Center a paper template on the wrong side of one fabric scrap and pin. Roughly trim the fabric into a hexagonal shape, leaving about ¼" seam allowance on all sides. **(4)**

3. Thread a hand-sewing needle with a contrasting color of thread that will be easy to see when it's time to remove it. Knot the end of the thread.

4. Fold the seam allowance over one side of the hexagon and bring the threaded needle through both layers of fabric and the paper template from the right side of the hexagon. Use a long stitch or two to baste the first side of the hexagon.

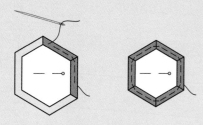

5. Continue onto the next side by folding the seam allowance over the template edge and basting in place with another long stitch or two. Work your way around the entire hexagon. When you reach the beginning leave a long tail of thread on the right side of the hexagon, but don't knot it. Repeat to prepare all the hexagons needed for your project. **(5)**

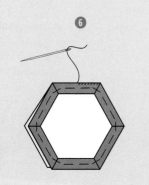

6. To sew the basted hexagons together, align two hexagons with right sides together. Thread a hand-sewing needle with a matching color or one that blends with both hexagons. Knot the thread tail and insert your needle between one paper template and the basted seam allowance of a hexagon, bringing your needle out at the folded edge to hide the knot. Use small whipstitches to join the hexagons along one side, catching only a couple of threads at each folded edge. Be sure you don't stitch through the paper template.

7. When you reach the end of the seam, open the two hexagons and check to be sure that the stitches are almost invisible from the right side and allow the hexagons to lie flat, side by side. Add a third hexagon to an adjacent edge of a joined hexagon and continue sewing one pair of edges at a time. **(6)**

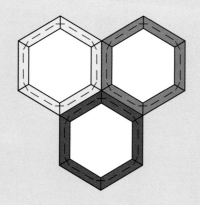

8. When all of the hexagons are sewn together, iron with a warm iron to set the edges. Snip and remove the basting threads and carefully pop out the paper template pieces.

MAKING THE TEA TOWEL

1. Layer the black-and-white 6" x 20½" rectangle on top of the linen 20½" x 30½" rectangle, right sides up, aligning the bottom raw edges. Baste in place ⅛" from the top and bottom edges of the black-and-white rectangle.

2. Center the pieced strip of hexagons along the top raw edge of the striped fabric and pin. Hand or machine stitch the strip of hexagons to the towel. **(7)**

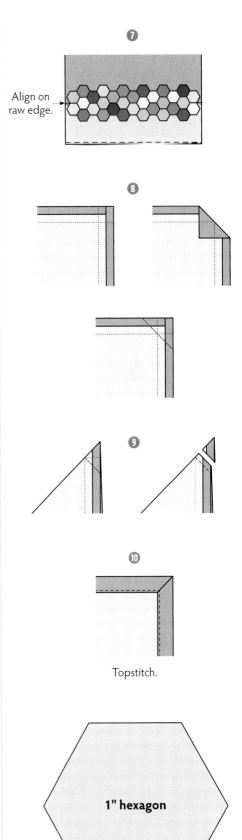

7

Align on raw edge.

••• Hold Tight •••

If you're appliquéing the towel hexagons by hand, use a quilting hoop or frame to hold the long layers of the tea towel taut while you stitch.

3. To begin the mitered hem, press ¼" to the wrong side on each of the four towel edges. Fold an additional ½" to the wrong side, press, and then open this fold. Fold a corner of the towel to the wrong side diagonally so that the creases of the second fold align through the corner. Press to crease the diagonal fold; then unfold and mark the diagonal crease with a removable fabric marker. **(8)**

4. Fold the towel diagonally with right sides together, aligning the outer edges and the marked line. Pin and then stitch on the marked line. Trim the corner, leaving ¼" seam allowances. Finger-press the seam allowances open. **(9)**

5. Turn the hemmed corner right side out and use a point turner, knitting needle, or chopstick to work the corners into place. Press the hem folds again to neaten. Repeat with the other three corners of the tea towel.

6. Pin the hem all around and topstitch close to the inner fold. **(10)**

8

9

10

Topstitch.

1" hexagon

All in a Row Table Runner

A cute little table runner adorned with rows of embroidered flowers is perfect for Mother's Day—or any spring occasion!

By Gail Pan

●●●

FINISHED RUNNER: 8½" x 21½"

MATERIALS

¼ yard *each* of cream tone on tone and dark-blue tone on tone for embroidered blocks and binding

⅛ yard *each* of blue floral, red floral, and green print

⅜ yard of fabric for backing

⅜ yard of 20"-wide lightweight fusible interfacing for embroidery backing

10" x 23" piece of batting

6-strand embroidery floss in pink, yellow, red, light blue, dark blue, light green, medium green, and dark green

Size 8 pearl cotton in ecru

CUTTING

From the cream tone on tone, cut:
2 rectangles, 5" x 10"

From the fusible interfacing, cut:
2 rectangles, 5" x 10"

From the blue floral, cut:
3 rectangles, 3½" x 8½"

From the red floral, cut:
2 rectangles, 2½" x 8½"

From the green print, cut:
2 rectangles, 1½" x 8½"

From the fabric for backing, cut:
1 rectangle, 10" x 23"

From the dark-blue tone on tone, cut:
2 strips, 2½" x 42"

EMBROIDERING THE DESIGNS

1. Center and transfer the design on page 48 onto the right sides of the two cream 5" x 10" rectangles using your preferred method. Iron the fusible interfacing to the wrong side of each rectangle.

2. Using two strands of floss, embroider the designs, using the stitches at right and following the embroidery key and color guides. **(1)**

1

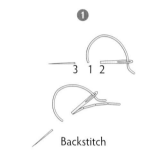
Backstitch

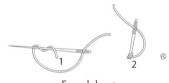
French knot

Lazy daisy

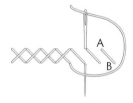
Cross-stitch

Satin stitch

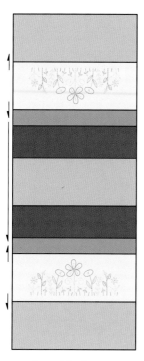

❷

Assembly diagram

ASSEMBLING THE RUNNER

1. Centering the embroidered design, trim each embroidered block to measure 8½" x 3½".

2. Sew the rectangles together as shown. Press the seam allowances in one direction; press the seam allowances away from the embroidered rectangles. **(2)**

3. Layer the runner top, batting, and backing; baste the layers together. Quilt with size 8 ecru pearl cotton, stitching ¼" from both sides of each seam, except on the embroidered panels.

> **••• Easy Quilting •••**
>
> Use ¼"-wide quilter's tape to guide your stitches without leaving marks that need to be erased or removed.

4. Trim the batting and backing to match the runner top.

5. Join the dark-blue 2½"-wide strips into a continuous length and use it to bind the table runner.

Embroidery Key

- • French knot
- ⌒ Lazy daisy
- ✕✕ Cross stitch
- ▨ Satin stitch
- — Backstitch

Needle Keeper

For years Jennifer parked hand-sewing needles in a scrap of wool tossed into her sewing basket. She decided to upgrade after admiring the many adorable needle cases her friends used. Torn between wool and cotton, she chose both. You can too! After all, once you have a cute needle case, you'll surely need more than one.

By Jennifer Keltner

● ● ●

FINISHED NEEDLE KEEPER:
2½" x 4" closed, 4" x 5" open

Wool Needle Keeper

MATERIALS

4½" x 6" piece of gold felted wool for exterior and center band

4½" x 5½" piece of teal felted wool for lining

3½" x 5" piece of cream felted wool for pages

12-weight wool embroidery thread or size 8 pearl cotton in teal

⅜ yard of ⅛"-diameter brown velvet cording

Scrap of freezer paper

CUTTING

From the gold felted wool, cut:
1 rectangle, 4" x 5"
1 strip, ½" x 4"

From the teal felted wool, cut:
1 rectangle, 4" x 5"

From the cream felted wool, cut:
1 rectangle, 3" x 4¼"

From the velvet cording, cut:
2 lengths, 6" each

ASSEMBLING THE CASE

1. Trace seven ½"-diameter circles (pattern on page 51) onto the matte side of freezer paper and cut out. Press the circles, shiny side down, onto the right side of the gold 4" x 5"

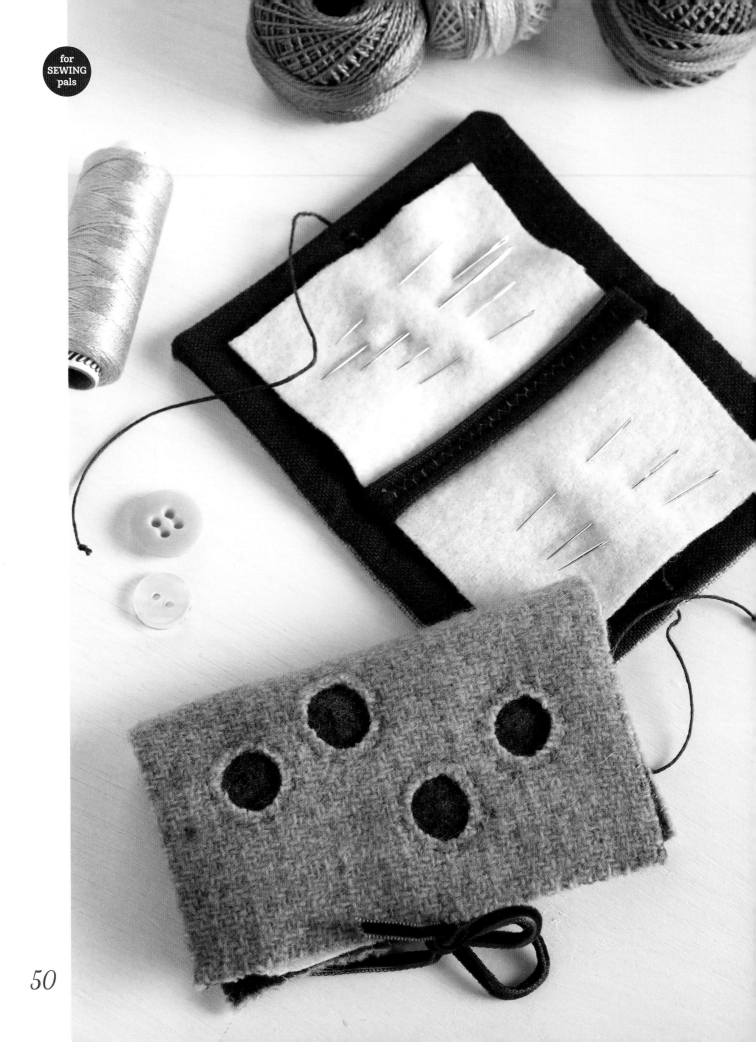

rectangle in the desired locations. Avoid placing circles too near the center fold line and edges of the case or too close together; allow at least ½" between circles. Once you're satisfied with the placement, trace around the circles with an air- or water-erasable fabric marker and carefully cut out each circle, snipping from the center out to the traced line for a clean, sharp edge.

••• Inner Circles •••

If you cut out the reverse appliqué circles carefully, you can use them to decorate the inside covers of your needle keeper. Place a few of them randomly on the lining and whipstitch the edges with matching thread, taking care that the stitches aren't visible on the exterior of the case.

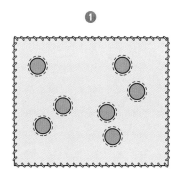

2. Layer the gold 4" x 5" rectangle on the teal rectangle, wrong sides together and aligning the raw edges. Whipstitch around the outer edges to join the pair.

3. Using a running stitch and one strand of wool thread, stitch around each cutaway circle, approximately ⅛" outside the cut edges. Be sure the stitches pass through both layers, and hide the thread tails between the layers. **(1)**

4. Fold the cream rectangle in half to measure 2⅛" x 3"; finger-press to crease. Unfold the cream rectangle and center the gold ½" x 4" strip over the crease, folding ½" of the strip to the back of the unit at each end. Baste the folded ends in place. **(2)**

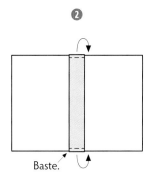

Baste.

5. Using light-colored tailor's chalk, draw a 4" line across the center of the teal lining. Align the center of the banded cream rectangle with the drawn line. Using a walking foot, sew a machine zigzag stitch (4.0 mm wide and 1.6 mm long) along the center of the gold band to join the layers. Remove the basting stitches. **(3)**

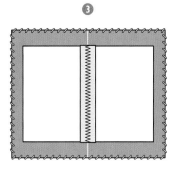

6. Knot one end of a 6" length of velvet cording. Tack the knot to the lining at the midpoint of one 4" edge, using matching thread and a few hand stitches. Repeat to secure the remaining piece of cording to the opposite edge of the lining.

Circle

Left: *Weave a decorative square on your needle case.*

Right: *Wool makes a perfect parking spot for pins and needles.*

Linen and Cotton Needle Keeper

MATERIALS

5" x 6" piece of natural linen for exterior

6" x 6" square of purple solid cotton for lining and center band

3½" x 5" piece of cream felted wool

⅜ yard of heavyweight waxed linen thread

12-weight wool embroidery thread or size 8 pearl cotton in purple

CUTTING

From the linen, cut:
1 rectangle, 4½" x 5½"

From the purple solid, cut:
1 rectangle, 4½" x 5½"
1 strip, 1" x 4"

From the cream felted wool, cut:
1 rectangle, 3" x 4¼"

From the waxed linen thread, cut:
2 lengths, 6" each

ASSEMBLING THE CASE

1. Arrange the linen rectangle horizontally on your work surface. Use an air- or water-erasable marker to draw a 1" square on the right side of the rectangle, 1" from the right and bottom edges. **(4)**

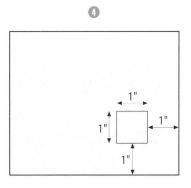

2. Using purple thread, sew 1"-long vertical straight stitches side by side to fill the drawn square. Space the stitches close together, but don't crowd the area. Bring the needle to the right side at one corner of the square. Leading with the needle eye instead of the point, weave a horizontal row from side to side by alternately passing over and under the vertical stitches across the entire square. Turn at the end of the row without passing through the fabric; if the finished row ends by passing over a vertical thread, begin the next row by passing under the same vertical thread, or vice versa. Repeat to weave as many horizontal rows as desired; the featured project has horizontal rows that fill approximately ⅔ of the 1" square. Pass the needle through the fabric when the weaving is complete and knot the thread on the wrong side to secure.

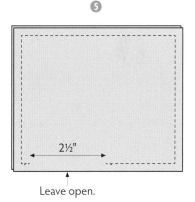

Leave open.

3. Pin the embellished linen rectangle and the purple 4½" x 5½" rectangle right sides together. Starting on one of the long edges and using a ¼" seam allowance, stitch all the way around the case, leaving a 2½" opening for turning. Backstitch at the beginning and end of the seam. **(5)**

4. Trim the corners diagonally and turn the case right side out through the opening. Press the cover, turning the seam allowances to the wrong side along the opening.

5. Press ¼" to the wrong side along each long edge of the 1" x 4" purple strip. Fold the cream wool rectangle in half; finger-press to crease. Open the wool rectangle and center the purple strip over the crease, folding ½" to the wrong side of the stack at each end. Baste the ends in place.

6. Draw a 4" line across the center of the purple lining. Align the center of the banded cream wool rectangle with the drawn line. Using a walking foot, machine stitch along the center of the purple band with a zigzag stitch 4.0 mm wide and 1.6 mm long.

7. Thread a tapestry needle with a 6" length of waxed linen thread and knot the end. Pass the needle through the case at the midpoint of one 4" edge from the lining side to the exterior. Unthread the needle and knot the remaining end of the thread. Repeat to secure the second length of linen thread to the opposite side of the needle case.

Woolly Pincushions

One of these pincushions is quick to make, and in groups they're especially charming. Make a few to share with all your stitch-loving friends.

By Fay Merritt Iseminger

• • •

FINISHED PINCUSHION:
3" diameter

MATERIALS

For each pincushion:

3½" x 7" piece of felted wool or flannel

Size 8 pearl cotton in matching or contrasting color

Cotton stuffing or polyester fiberfill

For buttons-and-ribbon pincushion:

1 button, 1¼" diameter

1 button, 1" diameter

Assorted ¼" buttons

7 mm-wide silk ribbon

For ruffled pincushion:

1 button, 1" to 1¼" diameter

1 to 3 buttons in graduated sizes from ½" to 1"

3½" x 7½" scrap of cotton print for ruffle

For lace pincushion:

1 button, 1" diameter

1 to 3 buttons in graduated sizes from ½" to ⅞"

¼ yard of 1"-wide lace edging

••• What Stuff? •••

It's OK to use any stuffing material you have on hand. The samples were made with cotton stuffing left over from upholstery projects. Polyester fiberfill is a readily available alternative. Wool is great for keeping pins rust-free, and you can stuff your pincushion with woolen yarn or project scraps if you like.

LA PEURLE

CUTTING

Circle pattern is on page 57.

From the felted wool, cut:

2 circles for each pincushion

EMBELLISHING THE PINCUSHIONS

Accent your pincushions with any combination of buttons, silk-ribbon embroidery, ruffles, and lace as shown in the photographs. Just pick and choose from the steps below.

Buttons-and-Ribbon Pincushion

1. Stack the buttons and sew them to the center of one felted-wool circle.

2. Use doubled all-purpose thread to sew about 20 small buttons in a random pattern around the edge of the center button. Don't space the buttons too tightly; leave room for the ribbon knots.

3. Cut 1 yard of silk ribbon and thread it into a large-eyed needle. Bring the ribbon to the right side of the circle, close to the edge of the center button and between two of the small buttons. Make a colonial knot as shown. Sew back down through the felted wool and bring the ribbon to the right side again between the next two buttons. Continue making colonial knots between the small buttons until there's a cluster of buttons and knots surrounding the center. (1)

Ruffled Pincushion

1. Cut a rectangle, 3" x 7", from the ruffle print. Press ¼" to the wrong side on each short end of the fabric rectangle. Fold the rectangle in half lengthwise, wrong sides together, and press.

2. Hand sew long running stitches or machine sew 4 to 5 mm-long stitches ⅛" from the raw edges of the pressed fabric. Pull the thread to gather the ruffle into a circle, overlapping the pressed ends slightly.

3. Center the ruffle on one felted-wool circle and tack it in place with a few hand stitches near the raw edges.

4. Sew the largest button to the center of the pincushion, hiding the raw edges of the ruffle. Stack and sew the other buttons on top.

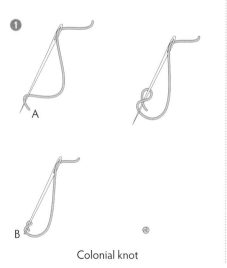

❶

A

B

Colonial knot

Lace Pincushion

1. Cut a 7" length of lace edging. Hand sew long running stitches or machine sew 4 to 5 mm-long stitches close to the straight lace edge. Pull the thread to gather the lace into a circle.

••• Love That Lace •••

Lace edging has one straight edge, with the other shaped into points or scallops. If you substitute lace with two straight edges or wider lace edging, you may need more than 7" for an attractive ruffle.

2. With right sides together, hand sew the ends of the lace in a ⅛" seam.

3. Center the gathered lace on one felted-wool circle and tack it in place with a few hand stitches along the straight edge.

4. Sew the largest button to the center of the pincushion, hiding the gathered lace edge. Stack the other buttons on top.

5. Stitch through the button stack from top to bottom, through the pincushion, leaving a long thread tail. Return through the pincushion and buttons through a different hole in the buttons. Tie the thread ends into a tiny bow and trim.

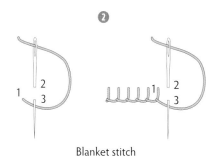

Blanket stitch

FINISHING THE PINCUSHION

1. Place the embellished pincushion circle on the second circle with wrong sides together. Use pearl cotton to sew the edges together with a running stitch ⅛" from the edge or sew blanket stitches that overcast the edge. Leave a 1" opening; don't tie off or cut the thread. (2)

2. Stuff the pincushion to the desired thickness.

3. Pick up the pearl cotton working thread and finish stitching the edges together.

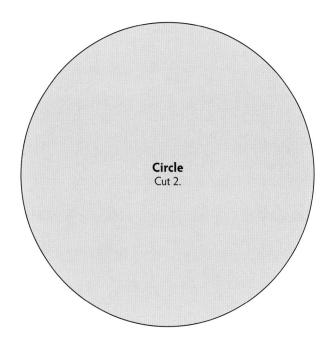

Circle
Cut 2.

Catcher in the Round

Whether you're stitching by hand or machine, thread tails and fabric bits pile up. Make this little catchall to rein in the mess. The little pocket holds your snips or an extra sewing-machine foot so you won't spend time patting the table, searching for these necessities.

By Jennifer Keltner

● ● ●

FINISHED CATCHER:

4" tall x 4" wide x 3" deep

MATERIALS

Fat eighths measure 9" x 21".

1 fat eighth *each* of salmon and green prints for bag exterior, lining, and pocket

1 fat eighth of teal print for binding

8½" x 16" piece of lightweight batting

CUTTING

From the salmon print, cut:
1 rectangle, 8½" x 16"

From the green print, cut:
1 rectangle, 8½" x 16"
1 rectangle, 2½" x 4½"

From the teal print, cut:
1 strip, 2½" x 14½"
1 strip, 2½" x 8"

QUILTING THE BAG

1. Make a quilt sandwich from the salmon rectangle, batting, and 8½" x 16" green rectangle. Smooth out the layers so that all of the edges are even. Pin at the corners, if desired, to hold the layers together and prevent shifting.

2. Using a ruler and an air- or water-erasable fabric-marking tool, draw an 8½"-long guideline through the widthwise center of the quilt sandwich. This line will be the guide for your first line of machine quilting.

A decorative stitch secures the binding.

3. Using a walking foot, machine quilt along the guideline. Using the width of your walking foot as a guide, machine quilt parallel rows back and forth across the entire rectangle, removing pins as you reach them. In the sample, the rows of quilting are ⅝" apart; vary that as you desire.

4. When the quilting is complete, trim the quilted rectangle to 7½" x 14½".

ASSEMBLING THE BAG

Stitch with a ¼" seam allowance.

1. Press the teal 2½" x 14½" strip in half lengthwise with wrong sides together. Align the raw edges of the folded strip with the top long edge of the quilted rectangle's lining fabric. Sew the binding to the top edge of the quilted rectangle.

2. Turn the binding to the front of the quilted rectangle. With the folded edge of the binding just covering the previous stitching line, machine stitch the binding in place with a straight or decorative stitch of your choice. The sample uses a machine blanket stitch.

3. Fold the green 2½" x 4½" rectangle in half, right sides together, to make a 2½" x 2¼" rectangle. Sew the two side seams. Trim the corners diagonally, turn the pocket right side out, and press.

4. Position the pocket on the quilted rectangle as shown, with the raw edge pointed up, and sew ¼" from the raw edge. Flip the pocket up to cover the seam allowances and press; then edgestitch each side edge of the pocket. **(1)**

5. Fold the quilted rectangle in half with the lining side out. Sew the short ends together, beginning at the bound edge, to make a tube.

6. Repeat step 1 to bind the seam using the teal 2½" x 8" strip. Before pressing the strip in half, press ½" to the wrong side at the upper edge so that there will be no raw edges visible. When you're finished, you'll have an open tube with binding around the top edge and covering the side seam. Leave the tube lining side out.

7. Flatten the tube with the side seam centered. Pin the raw edges together and sew the bottom seam. Mark the folds at each side with pins.

8. Fold the catcher so that the bottom seam is aligned with one marked side, making a point at the corner, and pin. Draw a line perpendicular to the seam 1½" from the tip of the triangle; sew along the line. Refold the catcher so that the second side is aligned with the bottom seam and repeat to box the second corner. Be sure you don't catch the bottom of the pocket in either boxing seam. **(2)**

9. Trim the excess fabric from each corner, leaving a ¼" seam allowance. Overcast or zigzag the raw edges if desired. Turn the catcher right side out. Fold 2" of the top edge to the outside, forming a cuff.

Directional prints are a great choice.

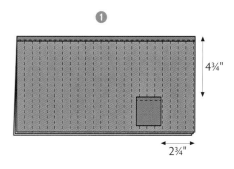

Biscornu Patchwork Pincushions

These pincushions are named for their unique shape; *biscornu* is a French word meaning *quirky* or *irregular*. Make one in an afternoon with either of the blocks described, or use your own favorite quilt block.

By Adrienne Smitke

● ● ●

FINISHED PINCUSHION:
6" x 6" x 2"

MATERIALS

Fat quarters measure 18" x 21"; fat eighths, 9" x 21".

For *each* pincushion:

Fiberfill or stuffing of your choice

Dollmaking needle

Embroidery floss or heavy-duty quilting thread

For the Star Pincushion:

⅛ yard *total* of assorted aqua prints for star

1 fat eighth of dark-blue print for background

1 fat eighth of teal dot for backing

1 button, ⅝" diameter

For the Four Corners Pincushion:

1 fat eighth of gray print for backing and center square

2 squares, 6" x 6", of assorted purple prints for top

2 squares, 6" x 6", of assorted orange prints for top

1 button, ¾" diameter

CUTTING

For the Star Pincushion:

From the assorted aqua prints, cut a *total* of:
1 square, 3½" x 3½"
8 squares, 2" x 2"

From the dark-blue print, cut:
4 rectangles, 2¼" x 3½"
4 squares, 2¼" x 2¼"

From the teal dot, cut:
1 square, 7" x 7"

For the Four Corners Pincushion:

From *each* of the 4 assorted purple and orange prints, cut:
1 rectangle, 2¾" x 3¾" (4 total)
1 rectangle, 1½" x 2¾" (4 total)

From the gray print, cut:
1 square, 2½" x 2½"
1 square, 7" x 7"

Make 4.

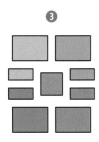

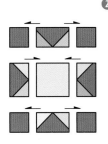

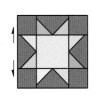

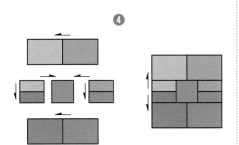

PIECING THE STAR BLOCK

1. Draw a diagonal line from corner to corner on the wrong side of each aqua 2" square. Place a marked square on a dark-blue 2¼" x 3½" rectangle, right sides together, aligning the bottom-left corners as shown. Sew on the drawn line. Trim the unit ¼" outside the sewn line and press the triangle and seam allowances toward the aqua piece. Repeat with a second aqua square on the bottom-right corner of the rectangle. Make four. **(1)**

••• Measure Up •••

The aqua squares in the Star block are slightly shorter than the height of the dark-blue rectangles. This moves the star's points away from the outer seams, for easy pincushion assembly.

2. Arrange the four units from step 1, the four dark-blue squares, and the remaining aqua square into rows as shown. Sew into rows and press the seam allowances toward the squares. Sew the rows together and press the seam allowances away from the center of the block. **(2)**

PIECING THE FOUR CORNERS BLOCK

1. Arrange the assorted purple and orange rectangles around the gray 2½" square as shown, keeping the large and small rectangles of the same fabric together. **(3)**

2. Sew the pieces into rows. Press the seam allowances in the top and bottom rows to one side and press the center row's seam allowances toward the gray square. Sew the rows together and press the seam allowances away from the center. **(4)**

ASSEMBLING THE PINCUSHIONS

1. Carefully square up a patchwork block as described in "Perfectly Square" on page 65. Trim the coordinating backing square to match.

••• Perfectly Square •••

In a perfect world, your patchwork block would always measure 7" x 7" after following the instructions, but nobody's perfect! When making a pincushion, it's important for your patchwork block to be a perfect square and *exactly* the same size as the backing square, so trim as needed to accomplish that goal. Adrienne trimmed both of her pieced blocks to 6¾" square.

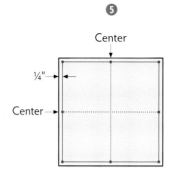

2. Baste a scant ⅛" around the outside of the pieced block to stabilize it and keep the seams from stretching.

3. Mark a ¼" seam allowance on the wrong side of *both* the patchwork block and the backing square. Make a small dot at each corner where the seamlines cross and at the center of each side. **(5)**

4. With right sides together, match the dot at one corner of the backing square with a dot at the center of one side of the patchwork block (A). Stick a straight pin through both dots to be sure they're aligned, and then use a second pin to hold the squares in place. **(6)**

5. Working clockwise, match up the next dot on the backing square (at a side's center) with the next dot on the patchwork block (at a corner). Pin as before (B). **(7)**

6. Make sure the fabric between the two dots is flat and aligned correctly, pinning as needed. Start sewing directly on the marked seamline about ¾" before the second dot (B), beginning with a few backstitches, and stop with the needle down when you reach the dot. Backstitch, then sew forward again to end with your needle down at the dot. This extra backstitching reinforces the corner during turning and stuffing. **(8)**

••• Clip Tip •••

You may find it helpful to make a small clip—just ⅛" to ³⁄₁₆" long—through the seam allowance at each side-center dot. The clip releases the seam allowance so that it opens up as you pivot around the corners.

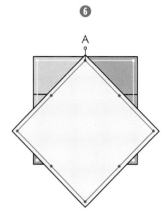

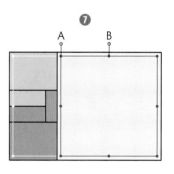

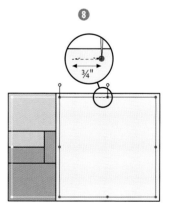

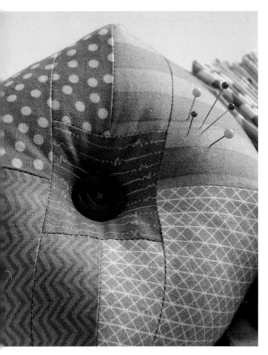

An indented button firms up the stuffing and adds extra style.

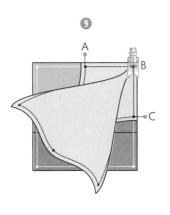

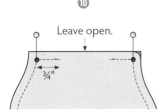

7. Keeping the needle down, lift the presser foot and pivot the entire pincushion counterclockwise so that you can continue sewing on the marked seamlines. Without removing the unit from the machine, match the next two dots (one corner and one side center), pinning to secure. Be sure that the fabric between the dots is aligned correctly and without wrinkles, and the additional fabric from the blocks is out of the way. Sew the segment between the pins, again finishing by backstitching and ending with the needle down at the dot. **(9)**

8. Repeat the process of matching up dots, sewing, and pivoting until you have worked all the way around the squares and are back at the first pinned pair of dots. Sew approximately ¾" past these dots and backstitch, leaving a gap at the center of the last side for turning and stuffing. **(10)**

9. Turn the pincushion right side out through the gap in the seam. Run a knitting needle with a rounded end or a chopstick along the seam from the inside to smooth the seam and shape the corners. Stuff the pincushion with fiberfill or your preferred stuffing. Hand stitch the opening closed.

10. Repeat steps 1–9 to assemble the second pincushion.

FINISHING THE PINCUSHION

1. Use an acrylic ruler and removable fabric marker to mark the center of the pincushion on both top and bottom.

2. Thread a long dollmaking needle with six strands of embroidery floss or a double strand of heavy-duty quilting thread and knot the end.

3. Bring the threaded needle from the back of the pincushion to the front through the center points. Sew through a decorative button, and then stitch back through to the bottom of the pincushion.

4. Pull both thread tails tight to tuft the pincushion and tie a sturdy knot to secure. Stitch through the pincushion and button again for strength, if desired. Tie another knot and clip the thread tails close to the pincushion.

Modern Rose Shoulder Bag

This classic bag is slightly structured, with gently angled bottom corners and a flap with a magnetic-snap closure. The strap widens at the top to rest comfortably on your shoulder, and the Art Nouveau–inspired felt flower can decorate the bag or be worn as a brooch.

By Amy Struckmeyer

● ● ●

FINISHED BAG: 9½" x 11"; shoulder strap (including tabs) is 23" long

MATERIALS

Yardage is based on 42"-wide fabrics unless otherwise noted. Fat quarters measure 18" x 21".

½ yard of large-scale yellow print for bag exterior*

½ yard of pink print for lining

⅜ yard *OR* 1 fat quarter of gray print for strap and flap

6" x 6" square of pink wool felt for rose

1 yard of 20"-wide nonwoven, medium-weight fusible interfacing

⅔ yard of 20"-wide lightweight fusible interfacing (woven or nonwoven)

6-strand embroidery floss in yellow

1 magnetic snap, ½" or ¾"

2 D-rings, 1½"

1 bar pin back, 1" (optional)

* If you prefer a single-fabric bag, ½ yard is still sufficient for the exterior, strap, and flap.

CUTTING

Patterns are on pages 72–75.

From the yellow print, cut:
2 bodies, *on fold*
2 squares, 4" x 4"

From the pink print, cut:
2 bodies, *on fold*
1 flap, *on fold*
2 rectangles, 5" x 7"

From the gray print, cut:
2 straps, *on fold*
1 flap, *on fold*

From the medium-weight interfacing, cut:
2 bodies, *on fold*
1 flap, *on fold*
2 squares, 4" x 4"
2 squares, 1½" x 1½"

From the lightweight interfacing, cut:
1 flap, *on fold*
1 strap, *on fold*
1 rectangle, 5" x 7"

From the wool felt, cut:
1 *each* of petals A–E (see "Perfect Petals" on page 69)

••• Perfect Petals •••

Trace the patterns for petals A–E onto the dull side of a piece of freezer paper and cut out along the lines. Iron each petal template to the wool felt, cut along the outlines, and remove the freezer-paper templates.

PREPARING THE FABRIC

1. Trim ⅛" from each edge of the medium-weight interfacing pieces. Following the manufacturer's instructions, fuse the interfacing to the wrong sides of the yellow exterior body pieces, gray flap piece, and both yellow 4" squares.

2. Trim ⅛" from each edge of the lightweight interfacing pieces. Following the manufacturer's instructions, fuse the interfacing to the wrong sides of the pink lining flap piece, one gray exterior bag strap, and one pink 5" x 7" rectangle.

ASSEMBLING THE LINING

Stitch with a ¼" seam allowance unless otherwise noted.

1. Place the pink 5" x 7" rectangles right sides together and sew around all four edges, leaving a 3" opening along one long edge for turning.

2. Clip the corners and turn the pocket right side out. Press the pocket, pressing ¼" to the wrong side along the opening. Topstitch ⅛" from the completely sewn long edge to make the top of the interior pocket.

3. Center the pocket on the right side of one pink body-lining piece, 2" below the top raw edge. Pin the pocket in place and sew it to the lining, topstitching ⅛" from the side and bottom edges. **(1)**

4. Fold one pink body-lining piece with right sides together and pin the dart edges. Sew each dart ¼" from the raw edges, beginning at the outer edge and tapering gradually to stitch off the fabric at the fold. Cut the threads, leaving long thread tails, and tie a knot to secure the tip of the dart. Repeat with the second lining piece. Press the darts toward the center on one piece and away from the center on the second piece. **(2)**

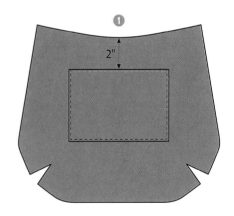

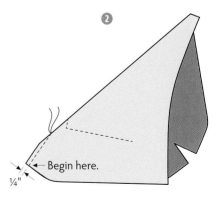

Begin here.
¼"

The shoulder bag looks fabulous in a single fabric, too.

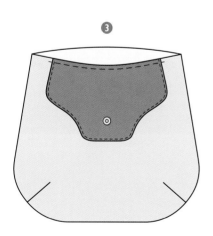

5. Pin the lining pieces right sides together with raw edges and darts aligned. Using a ½" seam allowance, sew the sides and bottom, leaving a 4" opening at the center of the bottom edge for turning. Clip the seam allowances along the curves; leave the lining wrong side out.

ASSEMBLING THE EXTERIOR AND FLAP

1. Fold one yellow body-exterior piece in half vertically and finger-press along the centerline. Open the body fabric and fuse a 1½" square of interfacing to the wrong side of the bag, centered on the crease 1¼" below the top edge.

2. Position one half of the magnetic snap on the right side of the bag body, centered on the crease 2" below the top raw edge. Install the magnetic snap following the manufacturer's instructions. This will be the bag front.

3. Pin the darts with right sides together and sew as you did for the lining. Repeat with the second yellow body-exterior piece. Press the darts toward the center on one piece and away from the center on the second piece.

4. Pin the exterior pieces right sides together with raw edges and darts aligned. Using a ½" seam allowance, sew the sides and bottom. Clip the seam allowances along the curves and turn the body right side out.

5. Fold the pink flap-lining piece in half vertically and finger-press along the centerline. Fuse a 1½" square of interfacing to the wrong side of the flap lining, centered on the crease ¾" above the bottom raw edge. Center the remaining half of the magnetic snap on the right side of the flap lining 1½" from the bottom raw edge. Install the magnetic snap following the manufacturer's instructions.

6. Pin the lining and exterior flaps right sides together and sew, leaving the top edge open. Clip the seam allowances along the curves, turn right side out, and press. Topstitch ⅛" from the sewn edges.

7. Center and pin the bag flap to the back exterior (the one without the magnetic snap), right sides together and aligning the raw edges. Baste ¼" from the raw edges. **(3)**

PREPARING THE TABS

1. Fold one yellow 4" square in half wrong sides together and press. Unfold the square and fold each raw edge in to align with the center crease; press again. Refold along the first crease and press again to make a 1" x 4" tab. Topstitch ⅛" from both long edges. Make two.

2. Feed each tab through a D-ring. Fold in half, matching the raw edges, and pin. **(4)**

3. Pin the tabs to the right side of the bag exterior, centering each one on a side seam with the raw edges aligned. Baste ¼" from the raw edges. **(5)**

FINISHING THE BAG

1. Place the bag exterior inside the lining with right sides together. Make sure the flap and tabs are tucked smoothly between the layers; match the seams and raw edges. Sew around the top of the bag using a ½" seam allowance. To reinforce the tabs, sew a second line of stitching over the tabs, ⅜" from the raw edges.

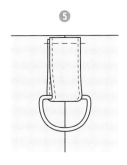

2. Turn the bag right side out through the opening in the lining. Sew the opening in the lining closed by hand or by machine.

3. Press the top edge of the bag and topstitch ¼" from the edge if desired.

4. Sew the strap pieces with right sides together along all sides, including the short ends, leaving a 3" opening at the center of one long side for turning. Trim the corners diagonally and clip the seam allowances along the curves. Turn the strap right side out and press, turning ¼" to the wrong side along the opening edges. Topstitch close to the edges, closing the gap as you sew.

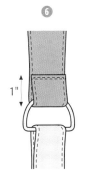

5. Feed one end of the strap through a D-ring from the outside. Fold 1" of the strap back on itself, wrong sides together, with the D-ring in the fold, and pin. Sew close to the short end of the strap through all layers. Repeat with the other end of the strap, making sure the strap is not twisted. **(6)**

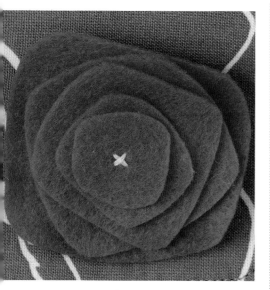

Make a felt rose to ornament the bag or your wardrobe.

MAKING THE ROSE

1. Stack the wool-felt petals with the largest on the bottom and the smallest on top. Rotate each shape until you're happy with the arrangement; for the sample, the arrangement is organic and not too ordered.

2. Using three strands of embroidery floss, hand stitch an X in the center of the rose, going over each stitch twice for extra reinforcement. Tie off securely in the back. There's no need to knot the end of the floss before stitching; instead, leave a long tail at the beginning and tie it to the end of the floss when the stitching is complete.

3. Hand sew the completed rose to the flap of the bag, sewing only through the bottom layer of felt and the exterior flap so that the stitches aren't visible.

••• Ramblin' Rose •••

As an option, sew or glue a bar pin to the back of the completed rose and pin the rose to the bag flap rather than stitching it there. With a bar pin, the rose doubles as a brooch. You can pin it on your sweater when you're not using the bag!

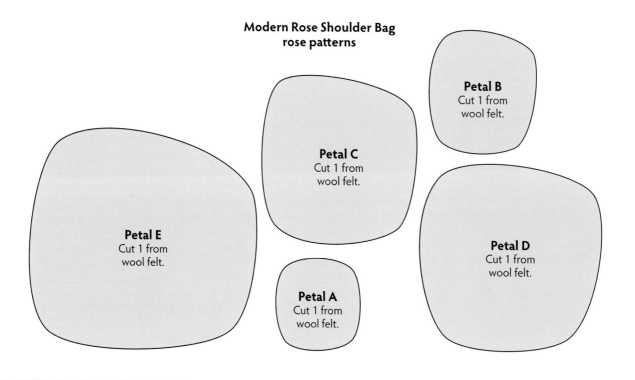

Modern Rose Shoulder Bag rose patterns

Petal B
Cut 1 from wool felt.

Petal C
Cut 1 from wool felt.

Petal E
Cut 1 from wool felt.

Petal D
Cut 1 from wool felt.

Petal A
Cut 1 from wool felt.

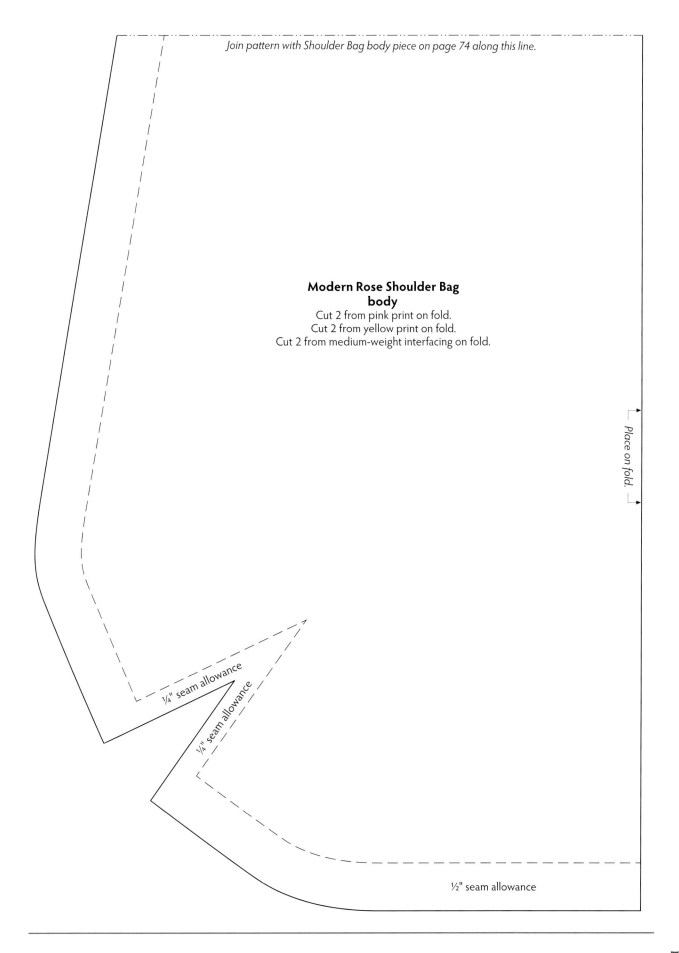

Join pattern with Shoulder Bag body piece on page 74 along this line.

Modern Rose Shoulder Bag
body
Cut 2 from pink print on fold.
Cut 2 from yellow print on fold.
Cut 2 from medium-weight interfacing on fold.

Place on fold.

¼" seam allowance

¼" seam allowance

½" seam allowance

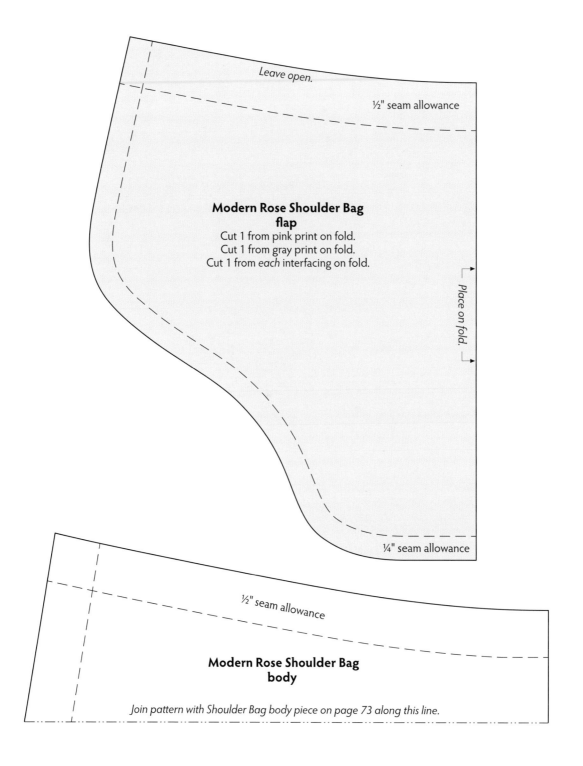

Leave open.

½" seam allowance

**Modern Rose Shoulder Bag
flap**
Cut 1 from pink print on fold.
Cut 1 from gray print on fold.
Cut 1 from *each* interfacing on fold.

Place on fold.

¼" seam allowance

½" seam allowance

**Modern Rose Shoulder Bag
body**

Join pattern with Shoulder Bag body piece on page 73 along this line.

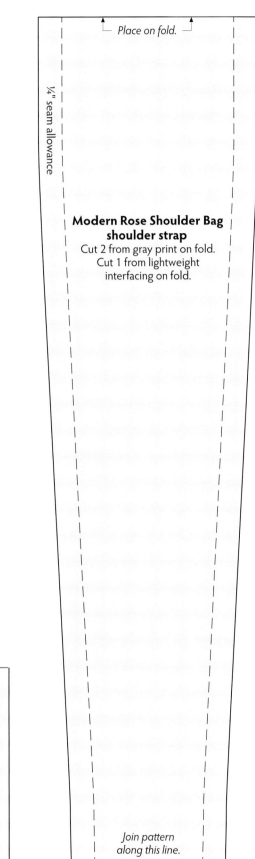

Place on fold.

¼" seam allowance

**Modern Rose Shoulder Bag
shoulder strap**
Cut 2 from gray print on fold.
Cut 1 from lightweight
interfacing on fold.

*Join pattern
along this line.*

*Join pattern
along this line.*

**Modern Rose
Shoulder Bag
shoulder strap**

Glam on the Go

The next time you give someone the gift of jewelry, tuck the gift into this little travel case. What a great surprise the recipient will have when she realizes you've given her more than a lovely handmade case!

By Natalie Barnes of beyond the reef

• • •

FINISHED CASE: 6½" x 6½" closed, 6½" x 18½" open

MATERIALS

Fat quarters measure 18" x 21".

6 fat quarters of assorted pink prints for cover and pocket linings

1 fat quarter of gray print for pockets and binding

1 fat quarter of white print for lining

8" x 20" piece of batting

2 zippers, 9" long

1 snap, ¾" diameter

CUTTING

From *each* of the assorted pink prints, cut:
4 rectangles, 1½" x 6½", for cover and ties (24 total)

From 2 of the pink prints, cut:
1 square, 6½" x 6½", for bracelet-pocket linings (2 total)

Continued on page 78.

••• Recipe for Colors and Fabrics •••

Select six coordinating fabrics you love, and use these for the strips that make up the cover of your travel case. Use the contrasting fabrics for the interior of the case.

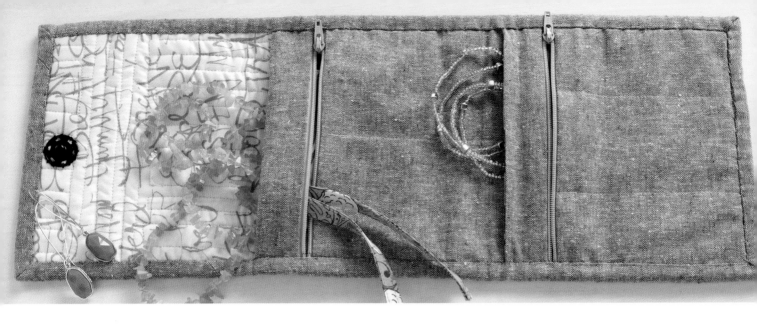

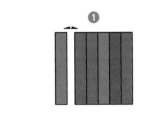

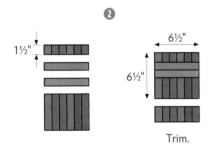

Continued from page 76.

From *2* of the pink prints, cut:
1 rectangle, 6½" x 12½", for necklace-pocket linings (2 total)

From the gray print, cut:
1 rectangle, 6½" x 12½", for necklace pocket
1 square, 6½" x 6½", for bracelet pocket
4 strips, 2¼" x 20", for binding

From the white print, cut:
1 rectangle, 8" x 20", for lining

MAKING AND QUILTING THE COVER

Stitch with a ¼" seam allowance. Your travel case is constructed in three sections—the cover, the large necklace pocket, and the smaller bracelet pocket.

1. Piece together six 1½" x 6½" strips to make a 6½" square. Press the seam allowances open. **(1)**

2. Cut across the vertical stripes 1½" from the top edge to create one 1½" x 6½" striped piece and one 5" x 6½" striped piece.

3. Sew two 1½" x 6½" strips together. Stitch the 1½" x 6½" pieced rectangle to one side of the unit and the 5" x 6½" pieced rectangle to the other side. Trim the larger pieced rectangle so that the entire unit measures 6½" x 6½". **(2)**

4. Sew twelve 1½" x 6½" strips to the original unit, working on the side with longer vertical stripes, to create a pieced exterior measuring 6½" x 18½". **(3)**

5. Make a quilt sandwich using the white 8" x 20" rectangle, batting, and pieced exterior. Quilt straight lines following the length of the strips and varying the spacing between lines of quilting. Trim the quilted cover to 6½" x 18½". (4)

MAKING THE POCKETS

1. Cut the gray 6½" square into two pieces, 1½" x 6½" and 5" x 6½". Using a zipper foot, install one zipper between the two sections of the square. The zipper is longer than the opening, so be sure to align the fabric pieces across the zipper tape. You'll trim the excess zipper later. Trim the larger side of the unit so that the entire unit measures 6½" x 6½". This is the bracelet pocket. (5)

2. Cut the gray 6½" x 12½" rectangle into two pieces, 1½" x 6½" and 11" x 6½". Install a zipper as you did in step 1. Trim the larger side of the unit so that the entire unit measures 6½" x 12½". This is the necklace pocket.

3. Press one remaining 1½" x 6½" strip in half lengthwise, wrong sides together. Open the fold and press each long edge to the wrong side so that the raw edges meet at the center crease. Refold along the center crease and press once more. Stitch along the center of each folded strip; tie a knot in one end of the strip. Make four ties. (6)

4. Place a pink 6½" square on the zippered unit from step 1, right sides together and matching the raw edges at the top of the zippered unit. Add a second pink 6½" square, placing its right side against the wrong side of the zippered unit. Stitch through all three layers along the edge parallel to the zipper. (7)

5. Flip both lining squares away from the zippered unit and press. Edgestitch the lining close to the seam. Fold the lining to the back of the zippered unit along the seam and press. Move the zipper pull to the center of the pocket, baste ⅛" from the side edges across the zipper ends, and trim the zipper to match the pocket edges.

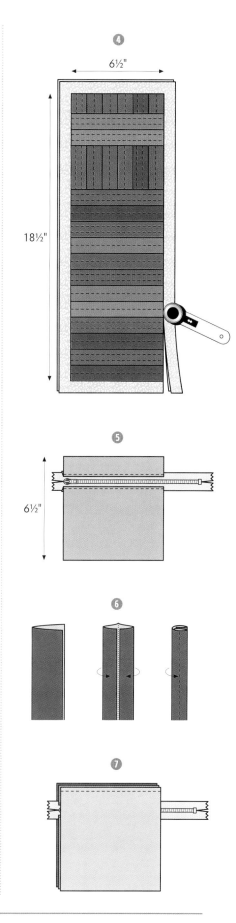

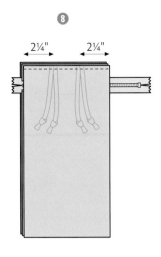

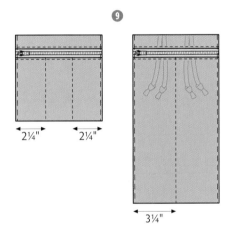

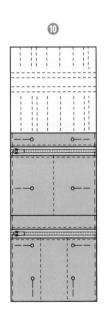

6. Mark the top edge of the necklace pocket 2¼" from each side edge. Baste the unknotted ends of two ties at each mark, stitching ⅛" from the raw edge. Repeat steps 4 and 5 to construct the pocket, using the pink 6½" x 12½" rectangles for the lining. Move the ties out of the way before edgestitching along the seam. **(8)**

7. Use a removable marking tool and a ruler to draw vertical lines across the bracelet pocket from the zipper to the bottom edge, 2¼" from each side edge. Stitch through all three layers of the pocket from the zipper to the bottom of the pocket, creating three compartments. Mark the vertical centerline of the necklace pocket and stitch from the zipper to the bottom edge to create two compartments. **(9)**

ASSEMBLING AND FINISHING

1. Place the necklace pocket on the lining side of the quilted cover, matching the side and bottom edges. Place the bracelet pocket on top, again matching the side and bottom edges. Baste or pin the layers together. **(10)**

2. Join the gray 2¼"-wide binding strips end to end to make one continuous length. Bind the outer edges of the jewelry case.

3. Stitch one half of the snap to the inside of the travel case, centered next to the binding on the end without pockets. Sew the second part of the snap to the outside of the case, centered 5" from the opposite end.

Go-To Tote

Make a sturdy, stylish tote that's the perfect size for carrying everyday essentials. It's also ideal for gift giving because it's fun and easy to customize for any recipient. Use a combination of durable fabrics, such as canvas and vinyl, and then add special details for a personalized touch.

By Beth Bradley

● ● ●

FINISHED TOTE: 15" tall x 9" wide x 4" deep

MATERIALS

Yardage is based on 42"-wide fabrics unless otherwise noted.

⅔ yard of blue canvas print for main panels

⅔ yard of peach solid for lining

¼ yard of 32-ounce faux-leather vinyl (pleather) for bottom

½ yard of fusible fleece

1 metal-toothed zipper, 14" long

Fabric clips, binder clips, or paper clips

Microfiber sewing-machine needle (optional)

Teflon presser foot (optional)

CUTTING

From the blue canvas print, cut:
2 rectangles, 14" x 18", for bag front and back*
2 strips, 4" x 21", for straps
2 rectangles, 1¼" x 2¼", for zipper tabs**

From the vinyl, cut:
2 rectangles, 6½" x 18", for bag bottom

From the peach solid, cut:
2 rectangles, 18" x 19½", for lining

From the fusible fleece, cut:
2 rectangles, 14" x 18"*
2 strips, 1¼" x 21"

If you plan to quilt the main bag panels, cut the canvas and fusible-fleece rectangles 1" larger on all sides to allow for shrinkage, and then trim the pieces to 14" x 18" after quilting.

**Measure your zipper's width before cutting and cut your pieces the zipper width x 2¼".*

PREPARING THE TOTE PIECES

Stitch with a ½" seam allowance unless otherwise noted.

1. Following the manufacturer's instructions, adhere the fusible-fleece rectangles to the wrong side of the bag front and back. If desired, add decorative quilting to the pieces, or customize them with decorative stitching or other embellishment. The sample has been quilted with wavy lines that echo the print.

2. Place one vinyl rectangle along the lower edge of the bag front with right sides together and hold the layers together with clips. Sew the pieces together; finger-press the seam allowances open. Topstitch the vinyl rectangle ⅛" from the seam. Repeat to assemble the bag back. **(1)**

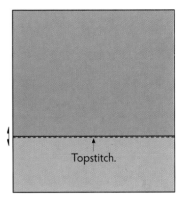

Topstitch.

Make 2.

> ### ••• Pleather Pointers •••
>
> Pleather is a form of vinyl that's treated to resemble the hand and texture of leather. It's a cinch to sew with a few special sewing tools and considerations.
>
> - Pins and needles make permanent holes in pleather, so use fabric or binder clips to hold the layers together before sewing.
>
> - Select a longer stitch length (3.0 to 4.0 mm) to avoid perforating the pleather too closely.
>
> - Use a fresh needle with a sharp point, such as a microfiber needle, to prevent skipped stitches on pleather.
>
> - If you find that your presser foot isn't gliding smoothly over the right side of the pleather when topstitching, switch to a Teflon presser foot or put masking tape on the underside of a standard foot.
>
> - Pleather has a plastic coating that will melt under heat, so finger-press seam allowances and creases instead of using an iron. Topstitch to hold the seam allowances in place in lieu of pressing with heat.

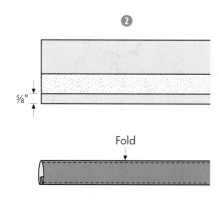

2

Fold

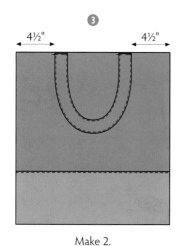

4½"   4½"

Make 2.

3

Topstitch.   Topstitch.

4

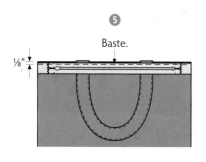

⅛" Baste.

5

6

3. Following the manufacturer's instructions, adhere one fusible-fleece strip to the wrong side of each strap piece, positioning the fleece ⅝" from one long edge of the fabric strap. Press ½" to the wrong side on both long edges of the straps. Fold the strap in half lengthwise with wrong sides together, matching the pressed edges and enclosing the fleece strips, and press. Topstitch ⅛" from both long edges. *Optional:* select a wide decorative stitch and sew lengthwise along the center of each strap; the sample uses a serpentine stitch. Make two straps. **(2)**

4. Position the ends of one strap along the top of the bag front, 4½" from the upper corners. Match the raw edges and make sure the strap isn't twisted. Pin; then baste the strap ends by stitching ¼" from the raw edges. Repeat to baste the remaining strap to the bag back. **(3)**

5. Press ¼" to the wrong side on one short end of each zipper tab. With right sides up, place the pressed tab edges on the ends of the zipper tape just outside the zipper stops. Stitch the tabs to the zipper by topstitching ⅛" from the pressed edges. **(4)**

ASSEMBLING THE TOTE

1. Place the zipper unit along the top edge of the bag front with right sides together. Baste the zipper unit to the bag ⅛" from the edge. **(5)**

2. Place one lining rectangle on the bag front, right sides together, sandwiching the zipper and straps between the layers. Sew the upper edge using a ¼" seam allowance. It's not necessary to use a zipper foot because the stitching isn't too close to the zipper teeth. **(6)**

3. Fold the bag and lining layers away from the zipper and the strap toward the zipper; press. Topstitch the bag front/lining ⅛" from the seam. **(7)**

4. Sew the bag back and second lining rectangle to the opposite long edge of the zipper tape, repeating steps 1–3. **(8)**

5. Unzip the zipper halfway; this is very important since you won't be able to turn the bag right side out if the zipper is closed. Refold the tote, matching the two lining pieces right sides together on one side of the zipper and the two exterior panels, also right sides together, on the other side of the zipper. Make sure the horizontal seams on the exterior pieces match at both side seams. Pin the fabric layers and clip the vinyl layers. Sew the entire perimeter of the bag, leaving a 9" opening along the lower edge of the lining for turning and backstitching securely at both sides of the opening. **(9)**

6. While the bag is still wrong side out, fold a lower corner of the bag exterior to align the side and bottom seams. Measure 2" from the corner and mark a line perpendicular to the seams. Stitch along the line to box the corner to add dimension to the bag. Trim the corners, leaving ½" seam allowances. Repeat to box the second lower corner of the bag exterior and both lower corners of the lining. **(10)**

7. Turn the bag right side out through the lining opening. Press the seam allowances along the opening to the wrong side and slip-stitch or edgestitch to close. Tuck the lining into the bag. Smooth all of the corners, including the ends of the zipper, into shape using a chopstick, point turner, or knitting needle.

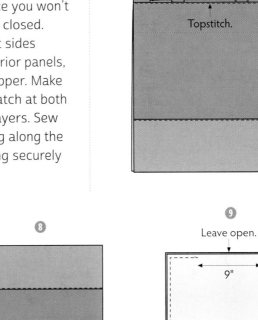

7

Topstitch.

8

Topstitch.

9

Leave open.

9"

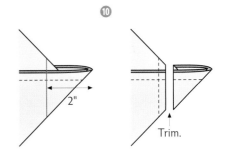

10

2"

Trim.

Cathedral Windows Pouch

Cathedral windows are a time-tested piecing tour de force, but stitched in modern fabrics they look oh, so au courant. Choose three fabrics for your window units, or dive into your scraps to create multicolored diamonds inside matching frames.

By Jamie Mueller

• • •

FINISHED POUCH: 7" x 11½"

MATERIALS

Fat quarters measure 18" x 21"; fat eighths, 9" x 21".

1 fat quarter of yellow print for window backgrounds

1 fat quarter of pink-and-yellow-swirl print for exterior and diamonds*

1 fat quarter of light-pink print for lining and frames

⅜ yard of 20"-wide woven fusible interfacing

1 zipper, 12" long

*If desired, fussy cut the exterior pieces and diamonds to feature different parts of the print.

CUTTING

From the yellow print, cut:
5 squares, 5" x 5"

From the pink-and-yellow-swirl print, cut:
5 squares, 1¼" x 1¼"
1 rectangle, 2½" x 12½"
1 rectangle, 3½" x 12½"
1 rectangle, 7½" x 12½"

From the light-pink print, cut:
5 squares, 2½" x 2½"
2 rectangles, 7½" x 12"

From the interfacing, cut:
1 rectangle, 2½" x 12½"
1 rectangle, 3½" x 12½"
1 rectangle, 7½" x 12½"

PREPARING THE FABRIC

Fuse the interfacing pieces to the wrong sides of the matching exterior pieces, following the manufacturer's instructions. Allow each piece to cool before proceeding.

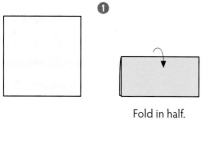

①

Fold in half.

Fold in half again; press.

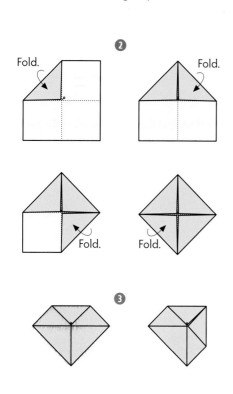

②

Fold.   Fold.

Fold.   Fold.

③

Fold in corners
to center; press.

④

Open folds,
center print
square on base.

Refold and
pin in place.

FOLDING THE CATHEDRAL WINDOWS

1. Finger-press a yellow square in half. Fold again in the opposite direction and finger-press once more to mark the centerlines. Open up the square and place a pin directly through the center, where the creases intersect. **(1)**

> ### ••• Spray Success •••
>
> Use a light spray of starch before each step of the folding process to keep the fabric stable and make it easier to work with. Use just a little, and take care when pressing; if your iron is too hot, the starch will make the fabric scorch easily. Test on a scrap first.

2. Fold one corner at a time to the center pin and press the crease. Repeat with all four corners. You'll have a smaller square with two fabric layers. **(2)**

3. Fold each new corner to the center and press. Repeat with all four corners. Pin the folded layers to hold them in place. Note that one side of the folded square will have all of the folded fabric, leaving the reverse side plain. Make five folded squares. **(3)**

SEWING THE WINDOWS

1. Open the top-layer flaps of a folded square and center a light-pink 2½" square on the folded unit, inside the creases. Refold the yellow square and pin the smaller square to the larger one through all the layers. **(4)**

2. With yellow thread in your sewing machine, take a few stitches vertically and horizontally across the four corners at the center of the square, forming a cross to tack down the points. Repeat for all five blocks. **(5)**

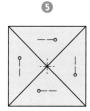

3. Set your sewing machine for a zigzag stitch 2.5 mm wide and 1.0 mm long. Place two prepared blocks side by side with their edges abutting and sew a zigzag along the edges. The left swing of the stitch should enter the left block and the right swing should pierce the right block. These stitches will be covered in the finished project, so don't be stressed about their appearance. Repeat to join all five folded squares in a row. **(6)**

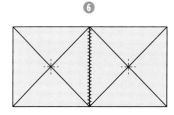

4. Position a 1¼" square on the diagonal so that it covers the zigzagged seam between the first two folded blocks and pin. Repeat to place three more 1¼" squares over the seams.

5. Cut the remaining 1¼" square in half diagonally. Place one triangle at each end of the pieced row as shown and pin. **(7)**

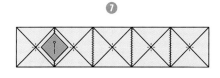

6. The folded edges of the yellow print are all on the bias, so they will fold and curve easily. Starting near one end of the pieced row where four corners come together (where they were tacked in step 2), fold each yellow edge toward the center of the 1¼" square. Pin the folded edge in place and repeat on all four sides of the 1¼" square. Work along the row until all of the curved edges are pinned, including two edges for each of the end triangles. The curving sides should cover the raw edges of the 1¼" squares and triangles. **(8)**

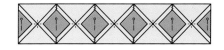

••• Pin Pointer •••

It's not really necessary to pin the curving edges before sewing, but Jamie recommends pins until you're fully comfortable with the technique.

Start here.

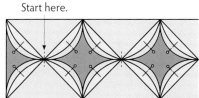

7. Pin the outer triangles along the top and bottom edges of the row in the same way. There's no contrasting fabric inside these triangles.

8. Starting near one end of the row where four corners come together, straight stitch near the edge of each folded window frame where it overlaps the 1¼" square. Sew the curved edges that don't enclose contrasting fabric in the same way, and edgestitch the free side of each end triangle. **(9)**

Start here.

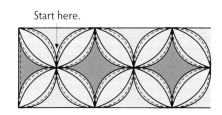

ASSEMBLING THE POUCH

Stitch with a ¼" seam allowance.

1. Sew the pink-and-yellow 2½" x 12½" rectangle to one long edge of the cathedral window row, sewing with right sides together and using a ¼" seam allowance on *both* pieces. Press the seam allowances toward the pink-and-yellow rectangle and topstitch ⅛" from the seam on the pink-and-yellow fabric. Repeat to stitch the pink-and-yellow 3½" x 12½" rectangle to the opposite side of the cathedral windows. **(10)**

2. Center the zipper on the assembled pouch front, right sides together and matching the upper edges. Place one lining rectangle, right side down, on the zipper; the right sides of the pouch and lining will be together with the zipper sandwiched between. Pin the layers and sew along the upper edge.

••• Zipper Tip •••

Using a zipper foot makes installing zippers much easier. If you don't have a zipper foot, move the zipper pull out of the way, repositioning it as necessary while you stitch along the zipper tape so that you can sew close to the zipper teeth.

⑩

3. Fold the pouch and lining away from the zipper, wrong sides together, and press. Topstitch ⅛" from the seam to secure the fabric layers and give the pouch a professional finish.

4. Repeat steps 2 and 3 to attach the pouch and lining backs to the opposite side of the zipper.

5. Open the zipper at least halfway. Don't skip this step or it will be impossible to turn the pouch right side out later!

6. Rearrange the pouch so that the exterior rectangles are right sides together on one side of the zipper and the lining rectangles are right sides together on the other side of the zipper. Pin the outer edges and sew around the entire pouch, leaving a 3" opening at the bottom of the lining for turning.

7. Trim the corners diagonally to reduce bulk, being careful not to cut the stitching. Turn the pouch right side out through the opening in the lining and the open zipper. Use a point turner or other tool to work the corners smoothly into place.

8. Close the opening in the lining with hand or machine stitches. Tuck the lining into the pouch exterior.

In the Clouds Patchwork Pouch

The soft colors of this quilted pouch are reminiscent of the diverse and unexpected colors in the sky on a cloudy day. The patchwork panel is a great way to turn trimmings from other projects into a pretty and practical gift.

By Adrienne Smitke

● ● ●

FINISHED POUCH: 8" x 4½" x 2½"

MATERIALS

Yardage is based on 42"-wide fabrics unless otherwise noted.

Assorted gray and pastel scraps, at least 1½" wide, for exterior

½ yard of blue polka dot for lining and binding

⅛ yard of gray linen/cotton blend for zipper panel

1 zipper, 14" long

15" x 16" piece of batting

¼ yard of ⅝"-wide gray ribbon for tabs

CUTTING

From the assorted scraps, cut:
Rectangles of various lengths, each 1½" wide, totaling about 150"
6 rectangles, 1½" x 3"

From the gray linen/cotton blend, cut:
2 strips, 1½" x 15½"

From the blue polka dot, cut:
1 rectangle, 9" x 12½"
2 strips, 1½" x 15½"
2 rectangles, 2½" x 3"
2 strips, 2¼" x 42"

From the batting, cut:
1 rectangle, 11" x 15"
2 squares, 5" x 5"

From the gray ribbon, cut:
2 pieces, 2½" long

Ribbon tabs add a neat functional finish.

PIECING THE EXTERIOR

Stitch with a ¼" seam allowance.

1. Arrange and piece the assorted 1½"-wide rectangles into nine rows, each at least 13" long. Press the seam allowances in one direction. Sew the rows together and press the seam allowances in one direction. **(1)**

2. Back the pieced panel with the 11" x 15" piece of batting and machine quilt as desired. The sample is quilted in straight lines that are stitched in the ditch of each vertical seam and ¼" to each side of those seams. **(2)**

3. Trim the quilted panel to 9" x 12½". Use the exterior-panel corner template on page 95 to round all four corners. Round the four corners of the polka-dot 9" x 12½" lining rectangle to match. **(3)**

This project is perfect for using up those last treasured scraps of a favorite fabric, like this Japanese linen cloud print.

①

At least 13"

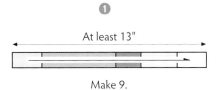

Make 9.

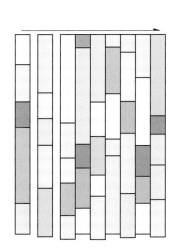

②

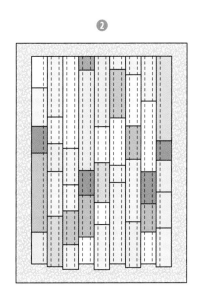

③

9"

12½"

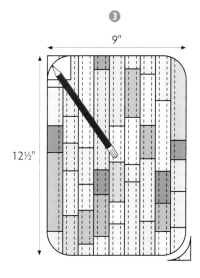

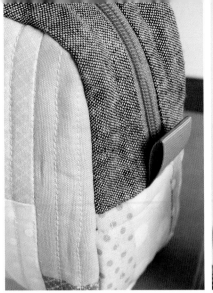

Make 2.

3"

2½"

Align top edges and stitch.

Topstitch.

4. For the side panels, sew three assorted 1½" x 3" rectangles side by side. Press the seam allowances in one direction. Make two. (4)

5. Back each side panel with a 5" square of batting and machine quilt to match the exterior panel. Trim the batting to match the patchwork, making two side panels, 3" x 2½" each. (5)

MAKING THE ZIPPER PANEL

1. Center the zipper along the length of a gray 1½" x 15½" strip, right sides together. Place a corresponding polka-dot strip on the unit, right side against the zipper's wrong side and aligning all three layers along the top edge. Pin together. Install a zipper foot on your machine and stitch the top edge. Press the fabrics away from the zipper and topstitch ¼" from the seam. (6)

2. Repeat step 1 to add the remaining gray and polka-dot 1½" x 15½" strips to the other side of the zipper. Trim the fabric even with the ends of the zipper tape on both ends.

3. Mark the zipper panel ¼" outside the top zipper stop. Fold a 2½" piece of ribbon in half and align the raw edges with the mark, positioning the fold over the zipper. Baste the ribbon to the zipper panel by stitching ⅛" from the ribbon ends. Basting will be easier if you move the zipper pull to the center of the zipper. (7)

••• Hand Basting •••

Because zipper tapes divide at each end, you may find it easier to baste the ribbon by hand.

4. Place a quilted side panel on the zipper panel, right sides together, with the ribbon between the layers. Align one 2½" edge of the side panel with the mark made in step 3 and pin. Turn the zipper unit over and place a polka-dot 2½" x 3" side lining on the unit with its right side against the zipper unit's wrong side. Match the edges of the lining rectangle to the quilted side panel. Using a zipper foot, stitch through all the layers ¼" from the raw edge of the side panel. Take care not to hit the zipper stops. Smooth the side panel and lining away from the zipper so that they are wrong sides together and press. Topstitch the side panels ¼" from the seam. Use the side-panel corner pattern at right to round the corners at the free end of the side panel. (8)

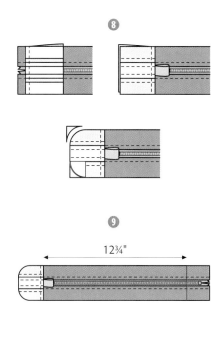

5. Measure and mark the zipper unit 12¾" from the seam attaching the side panel. Repeat steps 3 and 4, attaching the second ribbon, side panel, and lining. The zipper panel should finish 3" wide and 17" long, including seam allowances. (9)

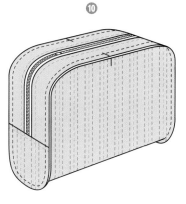

12¾"

ASSEMBLING THE POUCH

1. Layer the patchwork exterior panel and the polka-dot lining panel wrong sides together. Pin down the center of the panels to baste.

2. With a removable fabric-marking tool, mark the center of each side of the patchwork-panel lining and zipper panel.

3. *Make sure the zipper is partially unzipped.* With right sides together, match the centers of the zipper panel to the centers of the patchwork panel's short ends and pin. Match the center of each side panel to the center of a patchwork panel's long side and pin. Continue to pin the rest of the zipper/side panel unit to the patchwork panel, matching the raw edges and distributing the fabric evenly. Sew the zipper unit and patchwork panel together, working very carefully around the curves. Leave the pouch wrong side out and don't clip the seam allowances. (10)

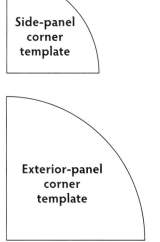

Side-panel corner template

Exterior-panel corner template

4. Join the polka-dot 2¼"-wide strips to make a continuous length and use it to bind the raw edges of the seam allowances. For more information on binding edges, go to ShopMartingale.com/HowToQuilt for free downloadable lessons.

5. Turn the pouch right side out through the open zipper.

About the Contributors

NATALIE BARNES is the owner of beyond the reef, a pattern-design company. You can find her at beyondthereefpatterns.com.

SARAH M. BISEL works hard to fit quilting time into her life. Check out her blog at MilkandHoneyDesigns.blogspot.com.

BETH BRADLEY earned a degree in Apparel Design and feels very lucky to have turned her fabric obsession into her livelihood, first as a clothing designer and now as an editor at Martingale. She loves spending the day surrounded by beautiful quilts, inspiring books, and incredibly gifted artists.

FAY MERRITT ISEMINGER is an artist who has been drawing all of her life. You can find her at Facebook.com/Made-by-Fay.

JENNIFER KELTNER has been a maker of things from a very early age. Her first truly independent crafting involved melting orange crayons in an Easy-Bake Oven—heated by a 20-watt lightbulb. She's passionate about all things fabric, quilting, embroidering, and sewing—always trying to squeeze a little "making" into every day.

ANDY KNOWLTON has been blogging at ABrightCorner.com since 2008 and enjoys teaching and sharing her love of color, fabric, and quilting.

JAMIE MUELLER learned to sew at a very early age. After graduating from Concordia University with a Bachelor of Arts degree, she became partners with her mother at Sunflower Quilts. They design patterns and notions, sell custom quilts, and offer machine quilting.

GAIL PAN lives on the outskirts of Melbourne, Australia, at the foothills of the beautiful Dandenong Ranges. In 2003, at the encouragement of some friends who were opening their own patchwork business, she began to design and release her own patterns.

AMY SMART is the author of the book *Fabulously Fast Quilts* and the blog Diary of a Quilter. She lives in Utah and loves to travel with her husband and four children. Visit her at DiaryofaQuilter.com.

ADRIENNE SMITKE grew up in a house full of handmade quilts and clothes. You can see more of Adrienne's patterns in the book *Everyday Handmade,* which she coauthored with her friend Cassie Barden, and in other Martingale compilations including *A Baker's Dozen, Quilting with Fat Quarters,* and *Sew Gifts!*

AMY STRUCKMEYER uses her design skills to create modern sewing projects and patterns, some of which have appeared in the books *Sew Gifts!* and *Kitchen Stitches.* Her book *A Bit of Appliqué* was released in 2015. Visit her at FormWorkDesign.blogspot.com.